THE YALE SHAKESPEARE

EDITED BY

WILBUR L. CROSS   TUCKER BROOKE
WILLARD HIGLEY DURHAM

PUBLISHED UNDER THE DIRECTION
OF THE
DEPARTMENT OF ENGLISH, YALE UNIVERSITY,
ON THE FUND
GIVEN TO THE YALE UNIVERSITY PRESS IN 1917
BY THE MEMBERS OF THE
KINGSLEY TRUST ASSOCIATION
TO COMMEMORATE THE SEVENTY-FIFTH ANNIVERSARY
OF THE FOUNDING OF THE SOCIETY

THE TRAGEDY OF CYMBELINE

EDITED BY

SAMUEL B. HEMINGWAY

NEW HAVEN · YALE UNIVERSITY PRESS

CONTENTS

The facsimile opposite reproduces the frontispiece to 'Cymbeline' in Rowe's edition of Shakespeare (1709).

[DRAMATIS PERSONÆ

CYMBELINE, *King of Britain*

CLOTEN, *Son to the Queen by a former Husband*

POSTHUMUS LEONATUS, *a Gentleman, Husband to Imogen*

BELARIUS, *a banished Lord, disguised under the name of Morgan*

GUIDERIUS
ARVIRAGUS
Sons to Cymbeline, disguised under the names of Polydore and Cadwal, supposed Sons to Morgan

PHILARIO, *Friend to Posthumus* ⎫
IACHIMO, *Friend to Philario* ⎬ *Italians*

A French Gentleman, *Friend to Philario*

CAIUS LUCIUS, *General of the Roman Forces*

A Roman Captain

Two British Captains

PISANIO, *Servant to Posthumus*

CORNELIUS, *a Physician*

Two Lords of Cymbeline's Court

Two Gentlemen of the same

Two Gaolers

QUEEN, *Wife to Cymbeline*

IMOGEN, *Daughter to Cymbeline by a former Queen*

HELEN, *a Lady attending on Imogen*

Lords, Ladies, Roman Senators, Tribunes, A Dutch Gentleman, A Spanish Gentleman, a Soothsayer, Musicians, Officers, Captains, Soldiers, Messengers, and other Attendants

Apparitions

SCENE: *Sometimes in Britain, sometimes in Rome*]

The Tragedy of Cymbeline

ACT FIRST

Scene One

[*Britain. The Garden of Cymbeline's Palace*]

Enter two Gentlemen.

1. Gent. You do not meet a man but frowns: our
bloods
No more obey the heavens than our courtiers
Still seem as does the king.

2. Gent.   But what's the matter?

1. Gent. His daughter, and the heir of 's kingdom,
whom   4
He purpos'd to his wife's sole son,—a widow
That late he married,—hath referr'd herself
Unto a poor but worthy gentleman. She's wedded;
Her husband banish'd; she imprison'd: all   8
Is outward sorrow, though I think the king
Be touch'd at very heart.

2. Gent.   None but the king?

1. Gent. He that hath lost her too; so is the queen,
That most desir'd the match; but not a courtier,   12
Although they wear their faces to the bent
Of the king's looks, hath a heart that is not
Glad at the thing they scowl at.

2. Gent.   And why so?

1. Gent. He that hath miss'd the princess is a
thing   16

1-3 our bloods . . . king; *cf. n.*   3 Still: *continually*
5 purpos'd: *intended to give in marriage*
6 referr'd: *committed*   13 to the bent: *according to the inclination*

Too bad for bad report; and he that hath her,—
I mean that married her, alack, good man!
And therefore banish'd—is a creature such
As, to seek through the regions of the earth   20
For one his like, there would be something failing
In him that should compare. I do not think
So fair an outward and such stuff within
Endows a man but he.

    2. Gent.   You speak him far.   24

    1. Gent. I do extend him, sir, within himself,
Crush him together rather than unfold
His measure duly.

    2. Gent.   What's his name and birth?

    1. Gent. I cannot delve him to the root: his father 28
Was called Sicilius, who did join his honour
Against the Romans with Cassibelan,
But had his titles by Tenantius whom
He serv'd with glory and admir'd success,   32
So gain'd the sur-addition Leonatus;
And had, besides this gentleman in question,
Two other sons, who in the wars o' the time
Died with their swords in hand; for which their
    father—   36
Then old and fond of issue—took such sorrow
That he quit being, and his gentle lady,
Big of this gentleman, our theme, deceas'd
As he was born. The king, he takes the babe   40
To his protection; calls him Posthumus Leonatus;
Breeds him and makes him of his bedchamber;
Puts to him all the learnings that his time
Could make him the receiver of; which he took,   44

22 him . . . compare: *him chosen for comparison*
24 speak him far: *go far in sounding his praise*
25 extend him within himself; *cf. n.*
29 join his honour: *honorably join*
33 sur-addition: *surname*

30, 31 *Cf. n.*
43 time: *years*

As we do air, fast as 'twas minister'd,
And in 's spring became a harvest; liv'd in court,—
Which rare it is to do,—most prais'd, most lov'd;
A sample to the youngest, to the more mature   48
A glass that feated them, and to the graver
A child that guided dotards; to his mistress,
For whom he now is banish'd, her own price
Proclaims how she esteem'd him and his virtue;   52
By her election may be truly read
What kind of man he is.

   2. Gent.   I honour him,
Even out of your report.   But pray you, tell me,
Is she sole child to the king?

   1. Gent.   His only child.   56
He had two sons,—if this be worth your hearing,
Mark it,—the eldest of them at three years old,
I' the swathing clothes the other, from their nursery
Were stol'n; and to this hour no guess in knowledge   60
Which way they went.

   2. Gent.   How long is this ago?

   1. Gent. Some twenty years.

   2. Gent. That a king's children should be so con-
     vey'd,
So slackly guarded, and the search so slow,   64
That could not trace them!

   1. Gent.   Howsoe'er 'tis strange,
Or that the negligence may well be laugh'd at,
Yet is it true, sir.

   2. Gent.   I do well believe you.

   1. Gent. We must forbear.   Here comes the gentle-
     man,   68

---

49 feated: *formed*
51 her own price: *what she is willing to pay in suffering*
53 election: *choice*   59 swathing: *swaddling*
60 guess in knowledge: *intelligent guess*
63 convey'd: *stolen*   68 forbear: *withdraw*

The queen, and princess.   *Exeunt.*

Enter the Queen, Posthumus, and Imogen.

Queen. No, be assur'd you shall not find me,
    daughter,
After the slander of most step-mothers,
Evil-ey'd unto you; you're my prisoner, but   72
Your gaoler shall deliver you the keys
That lock up your restraint.   For you, Posthumus,
So soon as I can win the offended king,
I will be known your advocate; marry, yet   76
The fire of rage is in him, and 'twere good
You lean'd unto his sentence with what patience
Your wisdom may inform you.
    Post.   Please your highness,
I will from hence to-day.
    Queen.   You know the peril: 80
I'll fetch a turn about the garden, pitying
The pangs of barr'd affections, though the king
Hath charg'd you should not speak together.   *Exit.*
    Imo.   O
Dissembling courtesy.   How fine this tyrant   84
Can tickle where she wounds!   My dearest husband,
I something fear my father's wrath; but nothing,—
Always reserv'd my holy duty,—what
His rage can do on me.   You must be gone;   88
And I shall here abide the hourly shot
Of angry eyes, not comforted to live,
But that there is this jewel in the world
That I may see again.
    Post.   My queen! my mistress!   92

69 S.d.; *cf. n.*   71 After the slander: *in accord with the ill repute*
78 lean'd: *should submit*   79 inform: *teach*
81 fetch a turn: *take a walk*
86 something: *somewhat*   nothing: *in no way*   84 fine: *delicately*
87 Always . . . duty; *cf. n.*

O lady, weep no more, lest I give cause
To be suspected of more tenderness
Than doth become a man.   I will remain
The loyal'st husband that did e'er plight troth.   96
My residence in Rome at one Philario's,
Who to my father was a friend, to me
Known but by letter; thither write, my queen,
And with mine eyes I'll drink the words you send,   100
Though ink be made of gall.

Enter Queen.

Queen.   Be brief, I pray you;
If the king come, I shall incur I know not
How much of his displeasure. [*Aside.*] Yet I'll move
          him
To walk this way.   I never do him wrong   104
But he does buy my injuries, to be friends
Pays dear for my offences.   [*Exit.*]
     Post.   Should we be taking leave
As long a term as yet we have to live,
The loathness to depart would grow.   Adieu!   108
     Imo. Nay, stay a little:
Were you but riding forth to air yourself
Such parting were too petty.   Look here, love;
This diamond was my mother's; take it, heart;   112
But keep it till you woo another wife,
When Imogen is dead.
     Post.   How! how! another?
You gentle gods, give me but this I have,
And cere up my embracements from a next   116
With bands of death!—Remain, remain thou here
                    [*Putting on the ring.*]

94 tenderness: *sensitiveness*   101 Though . . . gall; *cf. n.*
104-106 I never . . . offences; *cf. n.*   107 term: *period of time*
108 loathness: *reluctance*   116, 117 cere up . . . death; *cf. n.*

While sense can keep it on! And, sweetest, fairest,
As I my poor self did exchange for you,
To your so infinite loss, so in our trifles   120
I still win of you; for my sake wear this;
It is a manacle of love; I'll place it
Upon this fairest prisoner.

> [*Putting a bracelet on her arm.*]

   Imo.   O the gods!
When shall we see again?

> *Enter Cymbeline and Lords.*

   Post.   Alack! the king!   124
   Cym. Thou basest thing, avoid! hence, from my
    sight!
If after this command thou fraught the court
With thy unworthiness, thou diest.   Away!
Thou 'rt poison to my blood.
   Post. [*To Imogen*]   The gods protect you 128
And bless the good remainders of the court!
I am gone.   *Exit.*
   Imo.   There cannot be a pinch in death
More sharp than this is.
   Cym.   O disloyal thing,
That shouldst repair my youth, thou heap'st   132
A year's age on me.
   Imo.   I beseech you, sir,
Harm not yourself with your vexation;
I am senseless of your wrath; a touch more rare
Subdues all pangs, all fears.
   Cym.   Past grace? obedience? 136
   Imo. Past hope, and in despair; that way, past
    grace.

---

124 see: *meet*   125 avoid: *depart*
126 fraught: *burden (as of a ship)*
129 remainders: *those who remain*
135 a touch more rare: *a more precious emotion*

Cym. That mightst have had the sole son of my
　queen!

Imo. O bless'd, that I might not! I chose an eagle
And did avoid a puttock.　　　　　　　　　140

Cym. Thou took'st a beggar; wouldst have made my
　throne
A seat for baseness.

Imo.　　　　　No; I rather added
A lustre to it.

Cym.　　　　O thou vile one!

Imo.　　　　　　　　Sir,
It is your fault that I have lov'd Posthumus:　　144
You bred him as my playfellow, and he is
A man worth any woman, overbuys me
Almost the sum he pays.

Cym.　　　　　What! art thou mad?

Imo. Almost, sir; heaven restore me! Would I
　were　　　　　　　　　148
A neat-herd's daughter, and my Leonatus
Our neighbour shepherd's son!

Cym.　　　　　　　Thou foolish thing!

Enter Queen.

They were again together: you have done
Not after our command. Away with her,　　152
And pen her up.

Queen.　　　Beseech your patience. Peace!
Dear lady daughter, peace! Sweet sovereign,
Leave us to ourselves, and make yourself some comfort
Out of your best advice.

Cym.　　　　Nay, let her languish,　　156
A drop of blood a day; and, being aged,

---

140 puttock: *kite*　　　146, 147 overbuys me . . . pays; *cf. n.*
149 neat-herd's: *cowherd's*　　156 advice: *consideration*

Die of this folly!

                     Exit [*Cymbeline with Lords*].

Queen.   Fie! you must give way.

          Enter Pisanio.

Here is your servant. How now, sir! What news?
  Pis. My lord your son drew on my master.
  Queen.   Ha! 160
No harm, I trust, is done?
  Pis.   There might have been,
But that my master rather play'd than fought,
And had no help of anger; they were parted
By gentlemen at hand.
  Queen.   I am very glad on 't.   164
  Imo. Your son's my father's friend; he takes his
      part.
To draw upon an exile! O brave sir!
I would they were in Afric both together,
Myself by with a needle, that I might prick   168
The goer-back. Why came you from your master?
  Pis. On his command: he would not suffer me
To bring him to the haven; left these notes
Of what commands I should be subject to,   172
When 't pleas'd you to employ me.
  Queen.   This hath been
Your faithful servant; I dare lay mine honour
He will remain so.
  Pis.   I humbly thank your highness.
  Queen. Pray, walk awhile.
  Imo. [*To Pisanio.*] About some half-hour hence, 176
I pray you, speak with me. You shall at least
Go see my lord aboard; for this time leave me.

                         Exeunt.

171 bring: *escort*   176 walk: *withdraw*

Scene Two

[*The Same*]

Enter Cloten and two Lords.

1. Lord. Sir, I would advise you to shift a shirt; the violence of action hath made you reek as a sacrifice. Where air comes out, air comes in; there's none abroad so wholesome as that 4 you vent.

Clo. If my shirt were bloody, then to shift it. Have I hurt him?

2. Lord. [*Aside.*] No faith; not so much as 8 his patience.

1. Lord. Hurt him! his body's a passable carcass if he be not hurt; it is a throughfare for steel if it be not hurt. 12

2. Lord. [*Aside.*] His steel was in debt; it went o' the backside the town.

Clo. The villain would not stand me.

2. Lord. [*Aside.*] No; but he fled forward 16 still, toward your face.

1. Lord. Stand you! You have land enough of your own; but he added to your having, gave you some ground. 20

2. Lord. [*Aside.*] As many inches as you have oceans. Puppies!

Clo. I would they had not come between us. 24

2. Lord. [*Aside.*] So would I; till you had measured how long a fool you were upon the ground.

---

1 shift: *change*
10 passable: *affording passage*
13, 14 *Cf. n.*

2 reek: *steam*
11 throughfare: *thoroughfare*
15 stand: *withstand*

Clo. And that she should love this fellow and 28
refuse me!

2. Lord. [*Aside.*] If it be a sin to make a
true election, she is damned.

1. Lord. Sir, as I told you always, her 32
beauty and her brain go not together: she's a
good sign, but I have seen small reflection of her
wit.

2. Lord. [*Aside.*] She shines not upon fools, 36
lest the reflection should hurt her.

Clo. Come, I'll to my chamber. Would there
had been some hurt done!

2. Lord. [*Aside.*] I wish not so; unless it 40
had been the fall of an ass, which is no great
hurt.

Clo. You'll go with us?

1. Lord. I'll attend your lordship. 44

Clo. Nay, come, let's go together.

2. Lord. Well, my lord. *Exeunt.*

Scene Three

[*The Same*]

Enter Imogen and Pisanio.

Imo. I would thou grew'st unto the shores of the
haven,
And question'dst every sail: if he should write,
And I not have it, 'twere a paper lost,
As offer'd mercy is. What was the last 4
That he spake to thee?

Pis. It was his queen, his queen!

---

34 a good sign: *fair to look at*　　　　36, 37 *Cf. n.*
4 As offer'd mercy is; *cf. n*

Imo. Then wav'd his handkerchief?
Pis.　　　　　　　And kiss'd it, madam.
Imo. Senseless linen, happier therein than I!
And that was all?
Pis.　　　　　No, madam; for so long　　8
As he could make me with this eye or ear
Distinguish him from others, he did keep
The deck, with glove, or hat, or handkerchief,
Still waving, as the fits and stirs of 's mind　　12
Could best express how slow his soul sail'd on,
How swift his ship.
Imo.　　　　　Thou shouldst have made him
As little as a crow, or less, ere left
To after-eye him.
Pis.　　　　　Madam, so I did.　　16
Imo. I would have broke mine eye-strings, crack'd
　　them, but
To look upon him, till the diminution
Of space had pointed him sharp as my needle,
Nay, follow'd him till he had melted from　　20
The smallness of a gnat to air, and then
Have turn'd mine eye, and wept. But, good Pisanio,
When shall we hear from him?
Pis.　　　　　Be assur'd, madam,
With his next vantage.　　24
Imo. I did not take my leave of him, but had
Most pretty things to say; ere I could tell him
How I would think on him at certain hours
Such thoughts and such, or I could make him swear 28
The shes of Italy should not betray
Mine interest and his honour, or have charg'd him,
At the sixth hour of morn, at noon, at midnight,

15 left: *ceased*　　　　　　　　16 after-eye: *gaze after*
17 *Cf. n.*　　18, 19 diminution . . . space: *diminution due to space*
24 vantage: *opportunity*

To encounter me with orisons, for then　　　32
I am in heaven for him; or ere I could
Give him that parting kiss which I had set
Betwixt two charming words, comes in my father,
And like the tyrannous breathing of the north　　36
Shakes all our buds from growing.

Enter a Lady.

Lady.　　　　　　　　　The queen, madam,
Desires your highness' company.
　Imo. Those things I bid you do, get them dispatch'd.
I will attend the queen.　　　40
　Pis.　　　　　　Madam, I shall.　　*Exeunt.*

Scene Four

[Rome.　A Room in Philario's House]

*Enter Philario, Iachimo, a Frenchman, a Dutchman,
and a Spaniard.*

　Iach. Believe it, sir, I have seen him in
Britain; he was then of a crescent note, expected to prove so worthy as since he hath been
allowed the name of; but I could then have　4
looked on him without the help of admiration,
though the catalogue of his endowments had
been tabled by his side and I to peruse him
by items.　　　8
　Phi. You speak of him when he was less
furnished than now he is with that which makes
him both without and within.

32 encounter: *meet*　　　orisons: *prayers*　　　34-37 *Cf. n.*
35 charming: *having in them a charm to preserve him*
2 crescent note: *growing reputation*
5 admiration: *wonder*　　　7 tabled: *set down in a list*
10 furnished: *equipped*　　makes: *establishes*

French. I have seen him in France: we had 12 very many there could behold the sun with as firm eyes as he.

Iach. This matter of marrying his king's daughter,—wherein he must be weighed rather 16 by her value than his own,—words him, I doubt not, a great deal from the matter.

French. And then, his banishment.

Iach. Ay, and the approbation of those that 20 weep this lamentable divorce under her colours are wonderfully to extend him; be it but to fortify her judgment, which else an easy battery might lay flat, for taking a beggar without less 24 quality. But how comes it, he is to sojourn with you? How creeps acquaintance?

Phi. His father and I were soldiers together; to whom I have been often bound for no less 28 than my life. Here comes the Briton: let him be so entertained amongst you as suits, with gentlemen of your knowing, to a stranger of his quality.   32

Enter Posthumus.

I beseech you all, be better known to this gentleman, whom I commend to you, as a noble friend of mine; how worthy he is I will leave to appear hereafter, rather than story him in his own 36 hearing.

French. Sir, we have known together in Orleans.

Post. Since when I have been debtor to you 40

13, 14 *Cf. n.*   17, 18 words him . . . matter; *cf. n.*
20-22 the approbation . . . extend him; *cf. n.*
24, 25 without less quality: *with so little rank*   30 suits: *accords*
31 knowing: *experience*   36 story: *tell the story of*
38 known together: *known each other*

for courtesies, which I will be ever to pay and
yet pay still.

French. Sir, you o'er-rate my poor kindness.
I was glad I did atone my countryman and you; 44
it had been pity you should have been put
together with so mortal a purpose as then each
bore, upon importance of so slight and trivial a
nature.   48

Post. By your pardon, sir, I was then a young
traveller; rather shunned to go even with what I
heard than in my every action to be guided by
others' experiences; but, upon my mended judg- 52
ment,—if I offend not to say it is mended,—my
quarrel was not altogether slight.

French. Faith, yes, to be put to the arbitre-
ment of swords, and by such two that would by 56
all likelihood have confounded one the other, or
have fallen both.

Iach. Can we, with manners, ask what was
the difference?   60

French. Safely, I think. 'Twas a contention
in public, which may, without contradiction,
suffer the report. It was much like an argument
that fell out last night, where each of us fell 64
in praise of our country mistresses; this gentleman at that time vouching—and upon warrant
of bloody affirmation—his to be more fair, virtuous, wise, chaste, constant-qualified, and less 68
attemptable, than any the rarest of our ladies in
France.

41 ever to pay: *ever under obligation to pay*   44 atone: *reconcile*
47 importance: *matter*   50-52 rather . . . experiences; *cf. n.*
57 confounded: *destroyed*   62, 63 which . . . report; *cf. n.*
65 country mistresses: *ladies of our own countries*
66, 67 upon . . . affirmation; *cf. n.*
68 constant-qualified: *endowed with constancy*
69 attemptable: *liable to seduction*

Iach. That lady is not now living, or this
gentleman's opinion by this worn out.   72

Post. She holds her virtue still and I my
mind.

Iach. You must not so far prefer her 'fore
ours of Italy.   76

Post. Being so far provoked as I was in
France, I would abate her nothing, though I
profess myself her adorer, not her friend.

Iach. As fair and as good—a kind of hand- 80
in-hand comparison—had been something too
fair and too good for any lady in Britain. If she
went before others I have seen, as that diamond
of yours outlustres many I have beheld, I could 84
not but believe she excelled many; but I have
not seen the most precious diamond that is, nor
you the lady.

Post. I praised her as I rated her; so do I 88
my stone.

Iach. What do you esteem it at?

Post. More than the world enjoys.

Iach. Either your unparagoned mistress is 92
dead, or she's outprized by a trifle.

Post. You are mistaken; the one may be
sold, or given; or if there were wealth enough
for the purchase, or merit for the gift; the other 96
is not a thing for sale, and only the gift of the
gods.

Iach. Which the gods have given you?

Post. Which, by their graces, I will keep.   100

Iach. You may wear her in title yours, but,
you know, strange fowl light upon neighbouring

78 abate: *depreciate*   80 hand-in-hand: *equal*
88 rated her: *estimated her value*   91 enjoys: *possesses*
95, 96 or . . . or: *either . . . or*

ponds. Your ring may be stolen, too; so your
brace of unprizeable estimations, the one is but 104
frail and the other casual; a cunning thief, or a
that way accomplished courtier, would hazard
the winning both of first and last.

Post. Your Italy contains none so accom- 108
plished a courtier to convince the honour of my
mistress, if, in the holding or loss of that, you
term her frail. I do nothing doubt you have
store of thieves; notwithstanding I fear not my 112
ring.

Phi. Let us leave here, gentlemen.

Post. Sir, with all my heart. This worthy
signior, I thank him, makes no stranger of me; 116
we are familiar at first.

Iach. With five times so much conversation
I should get ground of your fair mistress, make
her go back, even to the yielding, had I admit- 120
tance and opportunity to friend.

Post. No, no.

Iach. I dare thereupon pawn the moiety of
my estate to your ring, which, in my opinion, 124
o'ervalues it something; but I make my wager
rather against your confidence than her reputation; and, to bar your offence herein too, I
durst attempt it against any lady in the world. 128

Post. You are a great deal abused in too bold
a persuasion; and I doubt not you sustain what
you're worthy of by your attempt.

Iach. What's that?   132

104 brace: *pair*   105 casual: *subject to chance*
109 convince: *conquer*   112 fear not: *fear not for*
114 leave here: *stop at this point*
117 familiar at first: *friends from the beginning*
123 moiety: *half*   129 abused: *deceived*
130 persuasion: *belief*

Post. A repulse; though your attempt, as you call it, deserves more,—a punishment too.

Phi. Gentlemen, enough of this; it came in too suddenly; let it die as it was born, and, I pray you, be better acquainted. 136

Iach. Would I had put my estate and my neighbour's on the approbation of what I have spoke! 140

Post. What lady would you choose to assail?

Iach. Yours; whom in constancy you think stands so safe. I will lay you ten thousand ducats to your ring, that, commend me to the court where your lady is, with no more advantage than the opportunity of a second conference, and I will bring from thence that honour of hers which you imagine so reserved. 144 148

Post. I will wage, against your gold, gold to it: my ring I hold dear as my finger; 'tis part of it.

Iach. You are a friend, and therein the wiser. If you buy ladies' flesh at a million a dram, you cannot preserve it from tainting. But I see you have some religion in you, that you fear. 152

Post. This is but a custom in your tongue; you bear a graver purpose, I hope. 156

Iach. I am the master of my speeches, and would undergo what's spoken, I swear.

Post. Will you? I shall but lend my diamond till your return. Let there be covenants drawn between 's: my mistress exceeds in goodness the hugeness of your unworthy thinking; I dare you to this match. Here's my ring. 160

Phi. I will have it no lay. 164

---

139 approbation: *confirmation* 149 wage: *wager*
151 a friend; *cf. n.* 155 custom . . . tongue: *manner of speech*
158 undergo: *maintain* 164 lay: *wager*

Iach. By the gods, it is one. If I bring you no sufficient testimony that I have enjoyed the dearest bodily part of your mistress, my ten thousand ducats are yours; so is your diamond 168 too: if I come off, and leave her in such honour as you have trust in, she your jewel, this your jewel, and my gold are yours; provided I have your commendation for my more free entertain- 172 ment.

Post. I embrace these conditions; let us have articles betwixt us. Only, thus far you shall answer: if you make your voyage upon 176 her and give me directly to understand you have prevail'd, I am no further your enemy; she is not worth our debate: if she remain un- seduced,—you not making it appear otherwise,— 180 for your ill opinion, and the assault you have made to her chastity, you shall answer me with your sword.

Iach. Your hand; a covenant. We will have 184 these things set down by lawful counsel, and straight away for Britain, lest the bargain should catch cold and starve. I will fetch my gold and have our two wagers recorded.   188

Post. Agreed.

[*Exeunt Posthumus and Iachimo.*]

French. Will this hold, think you?

Phi. Signior Iachimo will not from it. Pray, let us follow 'em.   *Exeunt.* 192

171-173 provided . . . entertainment; *cf. n.*
175 articles: *written agreements*   187 starve: *die of cold*

Scene Five

[Britain.   Cymbeline's Palace]

Enter Queen, Ladies, and Cornelius.

Queen. Whiles yet the dew's on ground, gather
   those flowers:
Make haste; who has the note of them?
   1. Lady.   I, madam.
   Queen. Dispatch.   *Exeunt Ladies.*
Now, Master doctor, have you brought those drugs? 4
   Cor. Pleaseth your highness, ay; here they are,
      madam: *[Presenting a small box.]*
But I beseech your Grace, without offence,—
My conscience bids me ask,—wherefore you have
Commanded of me these most poisonous compounds, 8
Which are the movers of a languishing death,
But though slow, deadly?
   Queen.   I wonder, doctor,
Thou ask'st me such a question: have I not been
Thy pupil long?   Hast thou not learn'd me how   12
To make perfumes? distil? preserve? yea, so
That our great king himself doth woo me oft
For my confections?   Having thus far proceeded,—
Unless thou think'st me devilish,—is 't not meet   16
That I did amplify my judgment in
Other conclusions?   I will try the forces
Of these thy compounds on such creatures as
We count not worth the hanging,—but none human,—
To try the vigour of them and apply   21
Allayments to their act, and by them gather
Their several virtues and effects.
   Cor.   Your highness

2 note of: *directions concerning*
18 conclusions: *experiments*

12 learn'd: *taught*
21 vigour: *power*

Shall from this practice but make hard your heart;   24
Besides, the seeing these effects will be
Both noisome and infectious.

  Queen.   O! content thee.

Enter Pisanio.

[*Aside.*] Here comes a flattering rascal; upon him
Will I first work: he's for his master,   28
And enemy to my son. How now, Pisanio!
Doctor, your service for this time is ended;
Take your own way.

  Cor.   [*Aside.*] I do suspect you, madam;
But you shall do no harm.

  Queen.   [*To Pisanio.*] Hark thee, a word. 32

  Cor. [*Aside.*] I do not like her. She doth think she
  has
Strange lingering poisons; I do know her spirit,
And will not trust one of her malice with
A drug of such damn'd nature. Those she has   36
Will stupefy and dull the sense awhile;
Which first, perchance, she'll prove on cats and dogs,
Then afterward up higher; but there is
No danger in what show of death it makes,   40
More than the locking-up the spirits a time,
To be more fresh, reviving. She is fool'd
With a most false effect; and I the truer,
So to be false with her.

  Queen.   No further service, doctor, 44
Until I send for thee.

  Cor.   I humbly take my leave. *Exit.*

  Queen. Weeps she still, sayst thou? Dost thou
  think in time

---

26 content thee: *do not worry*   38 prove: *test*
40 show: *appearance*   43 effect: *outward manifestation*

She will not quench, and let instructions enter
Where folly now possesses? Do thou work: 48
When thou shalt bring me word she loves my son,
I'll tell thee on the instant thou art then
As great as is thy master; greater, for
His fortunes all lie speechless, and his name 52
Is at last gasp; return he cannot, nor
Continue where he is; to shift his being
Is to exchange one misery with another,
And every day that comes comes to decay 56
A day's work in him. What shalt thou expect,
To be depender on a thing that leans,
Who cannot be new built, nor has no friends,
So much as but to prop him?
  [*The Queen drops the box; Pisanio takes it up.*]
        Thou tak'st up 60
Thou know'st not what; but take it for thy labour:
It is a thing I made, which hath the king
Five times redeem'd from death; I do not know
What is more cordial: nay, I prithee, take it; 64
It is an earnest of a further good
That I mean to thee. Tell thy mistress how
The case stands with her; do 't as from thyself.
Think what a change thou chancest on, but think 68
Thou hast thy mistress still, to boot, my son,
Who shall take notice of thee. I'll move the king
To any shape of thy preferment such
As thou'lt desire; and then myself, I chiefly, 72
That set thee on to this desert, am bound
To load thy merit richly. Call my women;
Think on my words.   *Exit Pisanio.*
    A sly and constant knave,

47 quench: *cool down* 54 shift . . . being: *change . . . abode*
56 decay: *destroy* 58 *Cf. n.* 64 cordial: *reviving*
55 earnest: *first payment to bind a bargain* 69 to boot: *in addition*

Not to be shak'd; the agent for his master,   76
And the remembrancer of her to hold
The hand-fast to her lord.   I have given him that
Which, if he take, shall quite unpeople her
Of liegers for her sweet, and which she after,   80
Except she bend her humour, shall be assur'd
To taste of too.

Enter Pisanio and Ladies.

     So, so;—well done, well done.
The violets, cowslips, and the primroses
Bear to my closet.   Fare thee well, Pisanio: 84
Think on my words.

        Exeunt Queen and Ladies
 Pis.   And shall do:
But when to my good lord I prove untrue,
I'll choke myself; there's all I'll do for you. *Exit.*

Scene Six

[*The Same*]

Enter Imogen alone.

 Imo. A father cruel, and a step-dame false;
A foolish suitor to a wedded lady,
That hath her husband banish'd: O! that husband,
My supreme crown of grief! and those repeated
Vexations of it!   Had I been thief-stol'n,
As my two brothers, happy! but most miserable
Is the desire that's glorious: bless'd be those,
How mean so'er, that have their honest wills,
Which seasons comfort.   Who may this be?   Fie!

---

77 remembrancer: *reminder*   78 hand-fast: *marriage contrac*
80 liegers: *ambassadors* sweet: *lover*
81 bend her humour: *change her inclination*
6-9 most miserable . . . comfort; *cf. n.*

Enter Pisanio and Iachimo.

Pis. Madam, a noble gentleman of Rome,
Comes from my lord with letters.
  Iach.   Change you, madam?
The worthy Leonatus is in safety,   12
And greets your highness dearly.
         [*Presents a letter.*]
  Imo.   Thanks, good sir.
You are kindly welcome.
  Iach. [*Aside.*] All of her that is out of door most
  rich!
If she be furnish'd with a mind so rare,   16
She is alone the Arabian bird, and I
Have lost the wager. Boldness be my friend!
Arm me, audacity, from head to foot!
Or, like the Parthian, I shall flying fight;   20
Rather, directly fly.
  Imo. reads: 'He is one of the noblest note, to
  whose kindnesses I am most infinitely tied. Reflect
  upon him accordingly, as you value your trust. 24
          LEONATUS.'
So far I read aloud;
But even the very middle of my heart
Is warm'd by the rest, and takes it thankfully. 28
You are as welcome, worthy sir, as I
Have words to bid you; and shall find it so
In all that I can do.
  Iach.   Thanks, fairest lady.
What! are men mad? Hath nature given them eyes 32
To see this vaulted arch, and the rich crop

11 Change you: *do you change color?*
15 out of door: *outwardly visible*
17 alone: *without rival*   Arabian bird: *phœnix*
20 Parthian; *cf. n.*

Of sea and land, which can distinguish 'twixt
The fiery orbs above and the twinn'd stones
Upon the number'd beach? and can we not   36
Partition make with spectacles so precious
'Twixt fair and foul?

    Imo.   What makes your admiration?

    Iach. It cannot be i' the eye, for apes and monkeys
'Twixt two such shes would chatter this way and   40
Contemn with mows the other; nor i' the judgment,
For idiots in this case of favour would
Be wisely definite; nor i' the appetite,—
Sluttery to such neat excellence oppos'd   44
Should make desire vomit emptiness,
Not so allur'd to feed.

    Imo. What is the matter, trow?

    Iach.   The cloyed will,—
That satiate yet unsatisfied desire, that tub   48
Both fill'd and running,—ravening first the lamb,
Longs after for the garbage.

    Imo.   What, dear sir,
Thus raps you? are you well?

    Iach.   Thanks, madam, well.
[*To Pisanio.*] Beseech you, sir,   52
Desire my man's abode where I did leave him;
He's strange and peevish.

    Pis.   I was going, sir,
To give him welcome.   *Exit.*

    Imo. Continues well my lord? His health, beseech
      you?   56

    Iach. Well, madam.

34-38 which . . . foul; *cf. n.*   38 makes: *causes*
41 mows: *grimaces*   42 favour: *beauty*
43 definite: *free from hesitation*   44-46 *Cf. n.*
47 trow: *I wonder*   49 ravening: *ravenously devouring*
50 after: *afterwards*   51 raps: *transports*
53 Desire . . . abode: *ask my man to remain*
54 strange: *a stranger*

Imo. Is he dispos'd to mirth? I hope he is.

Iach. Exceeding pleasant; none a stranger there
So merry and so gamesome: he is called   60
The Briton reveller.

Imo.   When he was here
He did incline to sadness, and oft-times
Not knowing why.

Iach.   I never saw him sad.
There is a Frenchman his companion, one,   64
An eminent monsieur, that, it seems, much loves
A Gallian girl at home; he furnaces
The thick sighs from him, whiles the jolly Briton—
Your lord, I mean—laughs from 's free lungs, cries,
     'O!   68
Can my sides hold, to think that man, who knows
By history, report, or his own proof,
What woman is, yea, what she cannot choose
But must be, will his free hours languish for   72
Assured bondage?'

Imo.   Will my lord say so?

Iach. Ay, madam, with his eyes in flood with
     laughter:
It is a recreation to be by
And hear him mock the Frenchman; but, heavens
     know,   76
Some men are much to blame.

Imo.   Not he, I hope.

Iach. Not he; but yet heaven's bounty towards him
     might
Be us'd more thankfully. In himself, 'tis much;
In you,—which I account his beyond all talents,— 80
Whilst I am bound to wonder, I am bound

---

62 sadness: *seriousness*   63 sad: *serious*
66 furnaces: *exhales as from a furnace* 70 proof: *experience*
79 'tis much: *i.e. heaven's bounty is great* 80 talents: *treasures*

To pity too.
    Imo.   What do you pity, sir?
    Iach. Two creatures, heartily.
    Imo.   Am I one, sir?
You look on me: what wrack discern you in me   84
Deserves your pity?
    Iach.   Lamentable! What!
To hide me from the radiant sun and solace
I' the dungeon by a snuff!
    Imo.   I pray you, sir,
Deliver with more openness your answers   88
To my demands. Why do you pity me?
    Iach. That others do,
I was about to say, enjoy your—But
It is an office of the gods to venge it,   92
Not mine to speak on 't.
    Imo.   You do seem to know
Something of me, or what concerns me; pray you,—
Since doubting things go ill often hurts more
Than to be sure they do; for certainties   96
Either are past remedies, or, timely knowing,
The remedy then born,—discover to me
What both you spur and stop.
    Iach.   Had I this cheek
To bathe my lips upon; this hand, whose touch,   100
Whose every touch, would force the feeler's soul
To the oath of loyalty; this object, which
Takes prisoner the wild motion of mine eye,
Firing it only here; should I—damn'd then—   104
Slaver with lips as common as the stairs
That mount the Capitol; join gripes with hands

---

84 wrack: *ruin*   86 to hide me: *to hide oneself*
87 snuff: *candle*   95 doubting: *suspecting that*
97, 98 timely knowing . . . born; *cf. n.*   98 discover: *reveal*
103, 104 Takes prisoner . . . here; *cf. n.*   103 motion: *passion*

Made hard with hourly falsehood,—falsehood, as
With labour;—then by-peeping in an eye,   108
Base and illustrous as the smoky light
That's fed with stinking tallow; it were fit
That all the plagues of hell should at one time
Encounter such revolt.

Imo.   My lord, I fear,   112
Has forgot Britain.

Iach.   And himself.   Not I,
Inclin'd to this intelligence, pronounce
The beggary of his change; but 'tis your graces
That from my mutest conscience to my tongue   116
Charms this report out.

Imo.   Let me hear no more.

Iach. O dearest soul! your cause doth strike my heart
With pity, that doth make me sick.   A lady
So fair,—and fasten'd to an empery   120
Would make the great'st king double,—to be partner'd
With tom-boys hir'd with that self exhibition
Which your own coffers yield! with diseas'd ventures
That play with all infirmities for gold   124
Which rottenness can lend nature! such boil'd stuff
As well might poison poison!   Be reveng'd;
Or she that bore you was no queen, and you
Recoil from your great stock.

Imo.   Reveng'd!   128
How should I be reveng'd?   If this be true,—
As I have such a heart, that both mine ears
Must not in haste abuse,—if it be true,

108 by-peeping: *looking sidelong*   109 illustrous: *without lustre*
112 Encounter such revolt: *meet such apostasy*
113-117 Not I . . . out; *cf. n.*   120 empery: *empire*
121 Would . . . double: *which would double the greatest king's do-
main*   partner'd: *associated*
122 tom-boys: *wanton women*   self: *same*   exhibition:
allowance   123 ventures: *chance mistresses*
125 boil'd stuff: *women who have been in the sweating tubs for vene-
real disease*   128 Recoil: *fall away*

How should I be reveng'd?
   Iach.   Should he make me   132
Live like Diana's priest, betwixt cold sheets,
Whiles he is vaulting variable ramps,
In your despite, upon your purse? Revenge it.
I dedicate myself to your sweet pleasure,   136
More noble than that runagate to your bed,
And will continue fast to your affection,
Still close as sure.
   Imo.   What ho, Pisanio!
   Iach. Let me my service tender on your lips.   140
   Imo. Away! I do condemn mine ears that have
So long attended thee. If thou wert honourable,
Thou wouldst have told this tale for virtue, not
For such an end thou seek'st; as base as strange.   144
Thou wrong'st a gentleman, who is as far
From thy report as thou from honour, and
Solicit'st here a lady that disdains
Thee and the devil alike. What ho, Pisanio!   148
The king my father shall be made acquainted
Of thy assault; if he shall think it fit,
A saucy stranger in his court to mart
As in a Romish stew and to expound   152
His beastly mind to us, he hath a court
He little cares for and a daughter who
He not respects at all. What ho, Pisanio!
   Iach. O happy Leonatus! I may say.   156
The credit that thy lady hath of thee
Deserves thy trust, and thy most perfect goodness
Her assur'd credit. Blessed live you long!
A lady to the worthiest sir that ever   160

134 ramps: *harlots*   135 In your despite: *in scorn of you*
137 runagate: *renegade*
139 Still . . . sure: *always as secretly as faithfully*
142 attended: *listened to*   151 saucy: *lascivious*   mart: *traffic*
152 stew: *brothel*   157 credit . . . of: *confidence . . . in*

Country call'd his; and you his mistress, only
For the most worthiest fit.   Give me your pardon.
I have spoken this, to know if your affiance
Were deeply rooted, and shall make your lord   164
That which he is, new o'er; and he is one
The truest manner'd; such a holy witch
That he enchants societies into him;
Half all men's hearts are his.

    Imo.   You make amends. 168

    Iach. He sits 'mongst men like a descended god:
He hath a kind of honour sets him off,
More than a mortal seeming.   Be not angry,
Most mighty princess, that I have adventur'd   172
To try your taking of a false report; which hath
Honour'd with confirmation your great judgment
In the election of a sir so rare,
Which you know cannot err.   The love I bear him 176
Made me to fan you thus; but the gods made you,
Unlike all others, chaffless.   Pray, your pardon.

    Imo. All's well, sir.   Take my power i' the court for
    yours.

    Iach. My humble thanks.   I had almost forgot   180
To entreat your Grace but in a small request,
And yet of moment too, for it concerns
Your lord, myself, and other noble friends,
Are partners in the business.

    Imo.   Pray, what is 't? 184

    Iach. Some dozen Romans of us and your lord,
The best feather of our wing, have mingled sums
To buy a present for the emperor;
Which I, the factor for the rest, have done   188
In France; 'tis plate of rare device, and jewels

163 affiance: *confidence*
166 truest manner'd: *of the soundest morals*
167 into: *unto*   184 Are: *who are*   188 factor: *agent*

Of rich and exquisite form; their values great;
And I am something curious, being strange,
To have them in safe stowage.　May it please you　192
To take them in protection?

　Imo.　　　　　　　Willingly;
And pawn mine honour for their safety: since
My lord hath interest in them, I will keep them
In my bedchamber.

　Iach.　　　　　They are in a trunk,　　196
Attended by my men; I will make bold
To send them to you, only for this night;
I must aboard to-morrow.

　Imo.　　　　　O! no, no.

　Iach. Yes, I beseech, or I shall short my word　200
By lengthening my return.　From Gallia
I cross'd the seas on purpose and on promise
To see your Grace.

　Imo.　　　I thank you for your pains;
But not away to-morrow!

　Iach.　　　　O! I must, madam:　204
Therefore I shall beseech you, if you please
To greet your lord with writing, do 't to-night:
I have outstood my time, which is material
To the tender of our present.

　Imo.　　　　　I will write.　　208
Send your trunk to me; it shall safe be kept,
And truly yielded you.　You're very welcome.

　　　　　　　　　　　　　Exeunt.

191 curious: *anxious*
207 outstood: *outstayed*　　material: *important*
208 tender: *presentation*

ACT SECOND

Scene One

[Britain. Cymbeline's Palace]

Enter Cloten and two Lords.

Clo. Was there ever man had such luck!
when I kissed the jack, upon an up-cast to be
hit away! I had a hundred pound on 't; and
then a whoreson jackanapes must take me up 4
for swearing, as if I borrowed mine oaths of him
and might not spend them at my pleasure.

1. Lord. What got he by that? You have
broke his pate with your bowl. 8

2. Lord. [*Aside.*] If his wit had been like
him that broke it, it would have run all out.

Clo. When a gentleman is disposed to swear,
it is not for any standers-by to curtail his 12
oaths, ha?

2. Lord. No, my lord; [*Aside.*] nor crop
the ears of them.

Clo. Whoreson dog! I give him satisfaction! 16
Would he had been one of my rank!

2. Lord. [*Aside.*] To have smelt like a
fool.

Clo. I am not vexed more at anything in the 20
earth. A pox on 't! I had rather not be so
noble as I am. They dare not fight with me because of the queen my mother. Every Jack-slave
hath his bellyful of fighting, and I must go 24
up and down like a cock that nobody can match.

2, 3 when . . . away; *cf. n.*
4 whoreson jackanapes: *rascally coxcomb*   take me up: *scold me*
12, 14 curtail, crop; *cf. n.*   23 Jack-slave: *low fellow*

2. Lord. [*Aside.*] You are cock and capon
too; and you crow, cock, with your comb on.

Clo. Sayest thou?   28

2. Lord. It is not fit your lordship should
undertake every companion that you give offence to.

Clo. No, I know that; but it is fit I should 32
commit offence to my inferiors.

2. Lord. Ay, it is fit for your lordship
only.

Clo. Why, so I say.   36

1. Lord. Did you hear of a stranger that's
come to court to-night?

Clo. A stranger, and I not know on 't!

2. Lord. [*Aside.*] He's a strange fellow him- 40
self, and knows it not.

1. Lord. There's an Italian come; and
'tis thought, one of Leonatus' friends.

Clo. Leonatus! a banished rascal; and he's 44
another, whatsoever he be. Who told you of
this stranger?

1. Lord. One of your lordship's pages.

Clo. Is it fit I went to look upon him? Is 48
there no derogation in 't?

1. Lord. You cannot derogate, my lord.

Clo. Not easily, I think.

2. Lord. [*Aside.*] You are a fool, granted; 52
therefore your issues, being foolish, do not
derogate.

Clo. Come, I'll go see this Italian. What

26, 27 capon . . . comb on; *cf. n.*
30 undertake: *give satisfaction to*   companion: *rascal*
49 derogation: *disparagement*
50, 54 derogate: *do anything derogatory to rank or position, and
    (quibblingly) degenerate*
53 issues: *acts, (quibblingly) offspring*

I have lost to-day at bowls I'll win to-night of 56
him. Come, go.
   2. Lord. I'll attend your lordship.

Exit [*Cloten*].

That such a crafty devil as is his mother
Should yield the world this ass! a woman that   60
Bears all down with her brain, and this her son
Cannot take two from twenty for his heart
And leave eighteen. Alas! poor princess,
Thou divine Imogen, what thou endur'st   64
Betwixt a father by thy step-dame govern'd,
A mother hourly coining plots, a wooer
More hateful than the foul expulsion is
Of thy dear husband, than that horrid act   68
Of the divorce he'd make. The heavens hold firm
The walls of thy dear honour; keep unshak'd
That temple, thy fair mind; that thou mayst stand,
To enjoy thy banish'd lord and this great land!   72

Exeunt [*Lords*].

Scene Two

[*A Bedchamber; in one part of it a Trunk*]

Imogen [*reading*] *in her bed; a Lady* [*attending*].

   Imo. Who's there? my woman Helen?
   Lady.   Please you, madam.
   Imo. What hour is it?
   Lady.   Almost midnight, madam.
   Imo. I have read three hours then; mine eyes are
   weak;
Fold down the leaf where I have left; to bed: 4
Take not away the taper, leave it burning,

62 for his heart: *to save his life*   66 coining: *fabricating*
69 he: *i.e. Cloten*   4 left: *stopped*

And if thou canst awake by four o' the clock,
I prithee, call me. Sleep has seized me wholly.

> [*Exit Lady.*]

To your protection I commend me, gods!   8
From fairies and the tempters of the night
Guard me, beseech ye!

> *Sleeps. Iachimo [comes] from the trunk.*

Iach. The crickets sing, and man's o'er-labour'd
  sense
Repairs itself by rest. Our Tarquin thus   12
Did softly press the rushes ere he waken'd
The chastity he wounded. Cytherea!
How bravely thou becom'st thy bed, fresh lily,
And whiter than the sheets! That I might touch!   16
But kiss: one kiss! Rubies unparagon'd,
How dearly they do 't! 'Tis her breathing that
Perfumes the chamber thus; the flame of the taper
Bows toward her, and would under-peep her lids,   20
To see the enclosed lights, now canopied
Under these windows, white and azure lac'd
With blue of heaven's own tinct. But my design,
To note the chamber: I will write all down: 24
Such and such pictures; there the window; such
Th' adornment of her bed; the arras, figures,
Why, such and such; and the contents o' the story.
Ah! but some natural notes about her body,   28
Above ten thousand meaner moveables
Would testify, to enrich mine inventory.
O sleep! thou ape of death, lie dull upon her;
And be her sense but as a monument   32

12 Our Tarquin; *cf. n.*   13 press . . . rushes; *cf. n.*
14 Cytherea: *Venus*   17, 18 But kiss . . . do 't; *cf. n.*
22 windows: *eyelids*   22, 23 white . . . tinct; *cf. n.*
23 tinct: *color*   26 arras: *wall-tapestry*   figures: *carvings*
27 contents o' the story; *cf. n.*
32 sense: *perception*   monument: *effigy*

Thus in a chapel lying. Come off, come off ;—
[*Taking off her bracelet.*]

As slippery as the Gordian knot was hard!
'Tis mine; and this will witness outwardly,
As strongly as the conscience does within,   36
To the madding of her lord. On her left breast
A mole cinque-spotted, like the crimson drops
I' the bottom of a cowslip: here's a voucher;
Stronger than ever law could make: this secret   40
Will force him think I have pick'd the lock and ta'en
The treasure of her honour. No more. To what end?
Why should I write this down, that's riveted,
Screw'd to my memory? She hath been reading late   44
The tale of Tereus; here the leaf's turn'd down
Where Philomel gave up. I have enough:
To the trunk again, and shut the spring of it.
Swift, swift, you dragons of the night, that dawning 48
May bare the raven's eye! I lodge in fear;
Though this a heavenly angel, hell is here.
Clock strikes.

One, two, three: time, time!
Exit [*into trunk*].

Scene Three

[*An Ante-chamber adjoining Imogen's Apartments*]

Enter Cloten and Lords.

1. Lord. Your lordship is the most patient man in loss, the most coldest that ever turned up ace.

---

34 Gordian knot; *cf. n.*   38 cinque-spotted: *having five spots*
45 The tale of Tereus; *cf. n.*   48, 49 that . . . eye; *cf. n.*
50 this: *i.e. this's*   51 time; *cf. n.*   2, 3 turned up ace; *cf. n.*

Clo. It would make any man cold to lose.   4

1. Lord. But not every man patient after the noble temper of your lordship. You are most hot and furious when you win.

Clo. Winning will put any man into courage.   8 If I could get this foolish Imogen, I should have gold enough. It's almost morning, is 't not?

1. Lord. Day, my lord.

Clo. I would this music would come. I am 12 advised to give her music o' mornings; they say it will penetrate.

Enter Musicians.

Come on; tune. If you can penetrate her with your fingering, so; we'll try with tongue too: 16 if none will do, let her remain; but I'll never give o'er. First, a very excellent good-conceited thing; after, a wonderful sweet air, with admirable rich words to it: and then let her 20 consider.

SONG.

'Hark! hark! the lark at heaven's gate sings,
　　And Phœbus 'gins arise,
His steeds to water at those springs　　　　24
　　On chalic'd flowers that lies;
And winking Mary-buds begin
　　To ope their golden eyes:
With everything that pretty is,　　　　　　28
　　My lady sweet, arise:
　　　　Arise, arise!'

---

14 penetrate: *touch the heart*　　　　　23 Phœbus: *the sun*
25 chalic'd: *having cup-like blossoms*
26 winking: *with eyes shut*　　Mary-buds: *buds of marigolds*

So, get you gone. If this penetrate, I will consider your music the better; if it do not, it is 32
a vice in her ears, which horse-hairs and calves'-guts, nor the voice of unpaved eunuch to boot,
can never amend.   [*Exeunt Musicians.*]

     2. Lord. Here comes the king.   36

     Clo. I am glad I was up so late, for that's the
reason I was up so early; he cannot choose but
take this service I have done fatherly.

Enter Cymbeline and Queen.

Good morrow to your majesty and to my 40
gracious mother.

Cym. Attend you here the door of our stern
     daughter?

Will she not forth?

     Clo. I have assail'd her with musics, but she 44
vouchsafes no notice.

Cym. The exile of her minion is too new,

She hath not yet forgot him; some more time

Must wear the print of his remembrance out,   48

And then she's yours.

     Queen.   You are most bound to the king,

Who lets go by no vantages that may

Prefer you to his daughter.   Frame yourself

To orderly soliciting, and be friended   52

With aptness of the season; make denials

Increase your services; so seem as if

You were inspir'd to do those duties which

You tender to her; that you in all obey her   56

Save when command to your dismission tends,

31, 32 consider: *requite*
33 horse-hairs: *fiddle-bows*   calves'-guts: *fiddle-strings*
34 unpaved: *unstoned, castrated*
46 minion: *favorite*   49 bound: *under obligation*
51 Prefer: *recommend*   Frame: *prepare*

And therein you are senseless.
    Clo.   Senseless! not so.

                [Enter a Messenger.]

   Mess. So like you, sir, ambassadors from Rome;
The one is Caius Lucius.
    Cym.   A worthy fellow,   60
Albeit he comes on angry purpose now;
But that's no fault of his: we must receive him
According to the honour of his sender;
And towards himself, his goodness forespent on us,   64
We must extend our notice.   Our dear son,
When you have given good morning to your mistress,
Attend the queen and us; we shall have need
To employ you towards this Roman.   Come, our queen.
                  Exeunt [all but Cloten].
    Clo. If she be up, I'll speak with her; if not,   69
Let her lie still, and dream.   By your leave, ho!
                      [Knocks.]
I know her women are about her.   What
If I do line one of their hands?   'Tis gold   72
Which buys admittance; oft it doth; yea, and makes
Diana's rangers false themselves, yield up
Their deer to the stand o' the stealer; and 'tis gold
Which makes the true man kill'd and saves the thief; 76
Nay, sometime hangs both thief and true man.   What
Can it not do and undo?   I will make
One of her women lawyer to me, for
I yet not understand the case myself.   80
By your leave.   *Knocks.*

58 senseless: *incapable of understanding*
59 So like you: *if it please you*
64 his goodness forespent: *because of his former goodness*
72 line: *put money into*
74 Diana's rangers: *forest-rangers of Diana, nymphs*   false: *betray*
75 stand: *station of huntsman waiting for game*   76 true: *honest*

Enter a Lady.

Lady. Who's there, that knocks?
Clo.   A gentleman.
Lady.   No more?
Clo. Yes, and a gentlewoman's son.
Lady.   [*Aside.*] That's more
Than some whose tailors are as dear as yours   84
Can justly boast of.   What's your lordship's pleasure?
Clo. Your lady's person: is she ready?
Lady.   Ay,
To keep her chamber.
Clo. There's gold for you; sell me your good
    report.   88
Lady. How! my good name? or to report of you
What I shall think is good?—The princess!

Enter Imogen.

Clo. Good morrow, fairest; sister, your sweet hand.
                              [*Exit Lady.*]
Imo. Good morrow, sir.   You lay out too much
    pains   92
For purchasing but trouble; the thanks I give
Is telling you that I am poor of thanks
And scarce can spare them.
Clo.   Still, I swear I love you.
Imo. If you but said so, 'twere as deep with me: 96
If you swear still, your recompense is still
That I regard it not.
Clo.   This is no answer.
Imo. But that you shall not say I yield being silent
I would not speak.   I pray you, spare me: faith,   100
I shall unfold equal discourtesy

82 No more?: *nothing else?*   92 lay out: *expend*
96 'twere as deep: *it would make as deep an impression*

To your best kindness. One of your great knowing
Should learn, being taught, forbearance.

    Clo. To leave you in your madness, 'twere my
    sin: 104
I will not.

    Imo. Fools cure not mad folks.

    Clo.   Do you call me fool?

    Imo. As I am mad, I do:
If you'll be patient, I'll no more be mad;   108
That cures us both. I am much sorry, sir,
You put me to forget a lady's manners,
By being so verbal; and learn now, for all,
That I, which know my heart, do here pronounce   112
By the very truth of it, I care not for you;
And am so near the lack of charity,—
To accuse myself,—I hate you; which I had rather
You felt than make 't my boast.

    Clo.   You sin against 116
Obedience, which you owe your father. For
The contract you pretend with that base wretch,
One bred of alms and foster'd with cold dishes,
With scraps o' the court, it is no contract, none;   120
And though it be allow'd in meaner parties—
Yet who than he more mean?—to knit their souls—
On whom there is no more dependancy
But brats and beggary—in self-figur'd knot;   124
Yet you are curb'd from that enlargement by
The consequence o' the crown, and must not foil
The precious note of it with a base slave,
A hilding for a livery, a squire's cloth,   128

111 verbal: *explicit*   123 dependancy: *consequence (of marriage)*
124 self-figur'd: *formed by themselves*
125 curb'd: *restrained*   enlargement: *liberty*
126 consequence: *succession*   foil: *pollute*
128 hilding: *rascal*   for: *fit only for*   squire's cloth: *lackey's
dress*

A pantler, not so eminent.
    Imo.   Profane fellow!
Wert thou the son of Jupiter, and no more
But what thou art besides, thou wert too base
To be his groom; thou wert dignified enough,   132
Even to the point of envy, if 'twere made
Comparative for your virtues, to be styl'd
The under-hangman of his kingdom, and hated
For being preferr'd so well.
    Clo.   The south-fog rot him! 136
    Imo. He never can meet more mischance than come
To be but nam'd of thee.   His meanest garment
That ever hath but clipp'd his body, is dearer
In my respect than all the hairs above thee,   140
Were they all made such men. How now, Pisanio!

                   Enter Pisanio.

    Clo. 'His garment!'   Now, the devil—
    Imo. To Dorothy my woman hie thee presently,—
    Clo. 'His garment!'
    Imo.   I am sprighted with a fool, 144
Frighted, and anger'd worse. Go, bid my woman
Search for a jewel that too casually
Hath left mine arm; it was thy master's, 'shrew me
If I would lose it for a revenue   148
Of any king's in Europe. I do think
I saw 't this morning; confident I am
Last night 'twas on mine arm, I kiss'd it;
I hope it be not gone to tell my lord   152
That I kiss aught but he.
    Pis.   'Twill not be lost.

129 pantler: *pantry servant*   132 dignified: *given dignity*
133, 134 made Comparative for: *compared with*
136 preferr'd: *advanced*   south-fog: *cf. n.*
139 clipp'd: *embraced*   144 sprighted with: *haunted by*

Imo. I hope so; go, and search.

[*Exit Pisanio.*]

Clo.   You have abus'd me:
'His meanest garment!'

Imo.   Ay, I said so, sir:
If you will make 't an action, call witness to 't.   156

Clo. I will inform your father.

Imo.   Your mother, too:
She's my good lady, and will conceive, I hope,
But the worst of me.   So I leave you, sir,
To the worst of discontent.

Clo.   I'll be reveng'd.   160
'His meanest garment!'   Well.   *Exit.*

Scene Fourth

[*Rome.   Philario's House*]

Enter Posthumus and Philario.

Post. Fear it not, sir; I would I were so sure
To win the king as I am bold her honour
Will remain hers.

Phi.   What means do you make to him?

Post. Not any, but abide the change of time,   4
Quake in the present winter's state and wish
That warmer days would come; in these fear'd hopes,
I barely gratify your love; they failing,
I must die much your debtor.   8

Phi. Your very goodness and your company
O'erpays all I can do.   By this, your king
Hath heard of great Augustus; Caius Lucius
Will do 's commission throughly, and I think   12

---

156 action: *law-suit*   2 bold: *confident*
3 means: *intercession*   4 abide: *await*
6-8 in these . . . debtor; *cf. n.*   12 throughly: *thoroughly*

He'll grant the tribute, send the arrearages,
Or look upon our Romans, whose remembrance
Is yet fresh in their grief.
    Post.   I do believe—
Statist though I am none, nor like to be—   16
That this will prove a war; and you shall hear
The legions now in Gallia sooner landed
In our not-fearing Britain, than have tidings
Of any penny tribute paid. Our countrymen   20
Are men more order'd than when Julius Cæsar
Smil'd at their lack of skill, but found their courage
Worthy his frowning at: their discipline,
Now mingled with their courage, will make known 24
To their approvers they are people such
That mend upon the world.
    Phi.   See! Iachimo!

Enter Iachimo.

    Post. The swiftest harts have posted you by land,
And winds of all the corners kiss'd your sails,   28
To make your vessel nimble.
    Phi.   Welcome, sir.
    Post. I hope the briefness of your answer made
The speediness of your return.
    Iach.   Your lady
Is one of the fairest that I have look'd upon.   32
    Post. And therewithal the best; or let her beauty
Look through a casement to allure false hearts
And be false with them.
    Iach.   Here are letters for you.

15 grief: *suffering*   16 Statist: *statesman*
17 prove: *turn out to be*   21 order'd: *disciplined*
24 mingled . . . courage; *cf. n.*
25 approvers: *those who make trial*
26 mend . . . world: *improve with experience*
27 posted: *conveyed swiftly*
28 corners: *quarters from which the wind blows*   30 made: *caused*

Post. Their tenour good, I trust.

Iach.   'Tis very like. 36

Phi. Was Caius Lucius in the Britain court
When you were there?

Iach.   He was expected then,
But not approach'd.

Post.   All is well yet.
Sparkles this stone as it was wont? or is 't not   40
Too dull for your good wearing?

Iach.   If I have lost it,
I should have lost the worth of it in gold.
I'll make a journey twice as far to enjoy
A second night of such sweet shortness which   44
Was mine in Britain; for the ring is won.

Post. The stone's too hard to come by.

Iach.   Not a whit,
Your lady being so easy.

Post.   Make not, sir,
Your loss your sport: I hope you know that we   48
Must not continue friends.

Iach.   Good sir, we must,
If you keep covenant.   Had I not brought
The knowledge of your mistress home, I grant
We were to question further, but I now   52
Profess myself the winner of her honour,
Together with your ring; and not the wronger
Of her or you, having proceeded but
By both your wills.

Post.   If you can make 't apparent 56
That you have tasted her in bed, my hand
And ring is yours; if not, the foul opinion
You had of her pure honour gains or loses
Your sword or mine or masterless leaves both   60

36 like: *probable*   47 easy: *compliant*   52 question: *debate*

To who shall find them.
 Iach.   Sir, my circumstances,
Being so near the truth as I will make them,
Must first induce you to believe: whose strength
I will confirm with oath; which, I doubt not, 64
You'll give me leave to spare, when you shall find
You need it not.
 Post.   Proceed.
 Iach.   First, her bedchamber,—
Where I confess I slept not, but profess
Had that was well worth watching,—it was hang'd 68
With tapestry of silk and silver; the story
Proud Cleopatra, when she met her Roman,
And Cydnus swell'd above the banks, or for
The press of boats or pride; a piece of work 72
So bravely done, so rich, that it did strive
In workmanship and value; which I wonder'd
Could be so rarely and exactly wrought,
Since the true life on 't was—
 Post.   This is true; 76
And this you might have heard of here, by me,
Or by some other.
 Iach.   More particulars
Must justify my knowledge.
 Post.   So they must,
Or do your honour injury.
 Iach.   The chimney 80
Is south the chamber, and the chimney-piece
Chaste Dian bathing; never saw I figures
So likely to report themselves; the cutter
Was as another nature, dumb; outwent her, 84
Motion and breath left out.

---

61 my circumstances: *details of my story* 68 watching: *wakefulness*
73 bravely: *excellently*   73, 74 strive . . . value; *cf. n.*
83 likely . . . themselves; *cf. n.*   83-85 the cutter . . . out; *cf. n.*

Post.   This is a thing
Which you might from relation likewise reap,
Being, as it is, much spoke of.
   Iach.   The roof o' the chamber
With golden cherubins is fretted; her andirons—   88
I had forgot them—were two winking Cupids
Of silver, each on one foot standing, nicely
Depending on their brands.
   Post.   This is her honour!
Let it be granted you have seen all this,—and praise 92
Be given to your remembrance,—the description
Of what is in her chamber nothing saves
The wager you have laid.
   Iach.   Then, if you can,
Be pale: I beg but leave to air this jewel; see!   96
                    [*Showing the bracelet.*]
And now 'tis up again; it must be married
To that your diamond; I'll keep them.
   Post.   Jove!
Once more let me behold it.   Is it that
Which I left with her?
   Iach.   Sir,—I thank her,—that: 100
She stripp'd it from her arm; I see her yet;
Her pretty action did outsell her gift,
And yet enriched it too.   She gave it me, and said
She priz'd it once.
   Post.   May be she pluck'd it off   104
To send it me.
   Iach.   She writes so to you, doth she?
   Post. O! no, no, no, 'tis true.   Here, take this too;
                    [*Gives the ring.*]

88 fretted: *embossed*   89 winking: *blind*
91 Depending: *leaning*   brands: *torches*
97 up: *put up*   102 outsell: *exceed in value*

It is a basilisk unto mine eye,
Kills me to look on 't.   Let there be no honour   108
Where there is beauty; truth where semblance; love
Where there's another man; the vows of women
Of no more bondage be to where they are made
Than they are to their virtues, which is nothing.   112
O! above measure false.
   Phi.   Have patience, sir,
And take your ring again; 'tis not yet won:
It may be probable she lost it; or
Who knows if one of her women, being corrupted,   116
Hath stol'n it from her?
   Post.   Very true;
And so I hope he came by 't.   Back my ring.
Render to me some corporal sign about her,
More evident than this; for this was stolen.   120
   Iach. By Jupiter, I had it from her arm.
   Post. Hark you, he swears; by Jupiter he swears.
'Tis true; nay, keep the ring; 'tis true: I am sure
She would not lose it; her attendants are   124
All sworn and honourable; they induc'd to steal it!
And by a stranger!   No, he hath enjoy'd her;
The cognizance of her incontinency
Is this; she hath bought the name of whore thus
      dearly.   128
There, take thy hire; and all the fiends of hell
Divide themselves between you!
   Phi.   Sir, be patient:
This is not strong enough to be believ'd
Of one persuaded well of—
   Post.   Never talk on 't;   132

107 basilisk: *fabulous serpent, said to kill with its look*
111 bondage: *binding force*   115 probable: *provable*
119 Render: *describe*   127 cognizance: *visible sign*
131 strong: *convincing*

She hath been colted by him.
    Iach.   If you seek
For further satisfying, under her breast,
Worthy the pressing, lies a mole, right proud
Of that most delicate lodging: by my life,   136
I kiss'd it, and it gave me present hunger
To feed again, though full. You do remember
This stain upon her?
    Post.   Ay, and it doth confirm
Another stain, as big as hell can hold,   140
Were there no more but it.
    Iach.   Will you hear more?
    Post. Spare your arithmetic; never count the turns;
Once, and a miliion!
    Iach.   I'll be sworn,—
    Post.   No swearing.
If you will swear you have not done 't, you lie;   144
And I will kill thee if thou dost deny
Thou 'st made me cuckold.
    Iach.   I'll deny nothing.
    Post. O, that I had her here, to tear her limb-meal!
I will go there and do 't, i' the court, before   148
Her father. I'll do something—   *Exit.*
    Phi.   Quite beside
The government of patience! You have won:
Let's follow him, and pervert the present wrath
He hath against himself.
    Iach.   With all my heart.   152
                              Exeunt.

137 present: *immediate*   147 limb-meal: *limb from limb*
151 pervert: *divert*

Scene Five

[*The Same.   Another Room*]

Enter Posthumus.

Post. Is there no way for men to be, but women
Must be half-workers? We are all bastards;
And that most venerable man which I
Did call my father was I know not where   4
When I was stamp'd; some coiner with his tools
Made me a counterfeit; yet my mother seem'd
The Dian of that time; so doth my wife
The nonpareil of this.   O! vengeance, vengeance;   8
Me of my lawful pleasure she restrain'd
And pray'd me oft forbearance; did it with
A pudency so rosy the sweet view on 't
Might well have warm'd old Saturn; that I thought
        her   12
As chaste as unsunn'd snow.   O! all the devils!
This yellow Iachimo, in an hour,—was 't not?
Or less—at first?—perchance he spoke not, but
Like a full-acorn'd boar, a German one,   16
Cried 'O!' and mounted; found no opposition
But what he look'd for should oppose and she
Should from encounter guard.   Could I find out
The woman's part in me!   For there's no motion   20
That tends to vice in man but I affirm
It is the woman's part; be it lying, note it,
The woman's; flattering, hers; deceiving, hers;
Lust and rank thoughts, hers, hers; revenges, hers; 24
Ambitions, covetings, change of prides, disdain,
Nice longing, slanders, mutability,
All faults that may be named, nay, that hell knows,

8 nonpareil: *one that has no equal*   11 pudency: *modesty*
20 motion: *impulse*   25 change: *variety*   26 Nice: *lascivious*

Why, hers, in part, or all; but rather, all;   28
For even to vice
They are not constant, but are changing still
One vice but of a minute old for one
Not half so old as that.   I'll write against them,   32
Detest them, curse them.   Yet 'tis greater skill
In a true hate to pray they have their will:
The very devils cannot plague them better.   *Exit.*

ACT THIRD

Scene One

[Britain.   Cymbeline's Palace]

*Enter in state, Cymbeline, Queen, Cloten, and Lords,
    at one door; and at another, Caius Lucius and
    Attendants.*

 Cym. Now say what would Augustus Cæsar with us?
 Luc. When Julius Cæsar—whose remembrance yet
Lives in men's eyes, and will to ears and tongues
Be theme and hearing ever—was in this Britain,   4
And conquer'd it, Cassibelan, thine uncle,—
Famous in Cæsar's praises, no whit less
Than in his feats deserving it,—for him
And his succession, granted Rome a tribute,   8
Yearly three thousand pounds, which by thee lately
Is left untender'd.
 Queen.   And, to kill the marvel,
Shall be so ever.
 Clo.   There be many Cæsars
Ere such another Julius.   Britain is   12

4 hearing: *tidings*

A world by itself, and we will nothing pay
For wearing our own noses.
      Queen.   That opportunity,
Which then they had to take from 's, to resume
We have again.   Remember, sir, my liege,   16
The kings your ancestors, together with
The natural bravery of your isle, which stands
As Neptune's park, ribbed and paled in
With oaks unscaleable and roaring waters,   20
With sands, that will not bear your enemies' boats,
But suck them up to the topmast.   A kind of conquest
Cæsar made here, but made not here his brag
Of 'came, and saw, and overcame': with shame—   24
The first that ever touch'd him—he was carried
From off our coast, twice beaten; and his shipping—
Poor ignorant baubles!—on our terrible seas,
Like egg-shells mov'd upon their surges, crack'd   28
As easily 'gainst our rocks: for joy whereof
The fam'd Cassibelan, who was once at point—
O giglot fortune!—to master Cæsar's sword,
Made Lud's town with rejoicing-fires bright,   32
And Britons strut with courage.
      Clo. Come, there's no more tribute to be paid.
Our kingdom is stronger than it was at that time;
and, as I said, there is no moe such Cæsars; 36
other of them may have crooked noses, but to
owe such straight arms, none.
      Cym. Son, let your mother end.
      Clo. We have yet many among us can gripe as 40
hard as Cassibelan; I do not say I am one, but I
have a hand.   Why tribute? why should we pay

18 bravery: *defiant spirit*   19 paled: *fenced*
20 oaks; *cf. n.*   27 baubles: *toys*
30 at point: *about*   31 giglot: *harlot*
32 Lud's town: *London*   36 moe: *more*   38 owe: *own*

tribute? If Cæsar can hide the sun from us with
a blanket, or put the moon in his pocket, we will 44
pay him tribute for light; else, sir, no more tribute, pray you now.

Cym. You must know,
Till the injurious Romans did extort   48
This tribute from us, we were free; Cæsar's ambition—
Which swell'd so much that it did almost stretch
The sides o' the world—against all colour here
Did put the yoke upon 's; which to shake off   52
Becomes a warlike people, whom we reckon
Ourselves to be. We do say then to Cæsar,
Our ancestor was that Mulmutius which
Ordain'd our laws, whose use the sword of Cæsar   56
Hath too much mangled; whose repair and franchise
Shall, by the power we hold, be our good deed,
Though Rome be therefore angry. Mulmutius made
        our laws,
Who was the first of Britain which did put   60
His brows within a golden crown, and call'd
Himself a king.

Luc.   I am sorry, Cymbeline,
That I am to pronounce Augustus Cæsar—
Cæsar, that hath more kings his servants than   64
Thyself domestic officers—thine enemy.
Receive it from me, then: war and confusion
In Cæsar's name pronounce I 'gainst thee: look
For fury not to be resisted. Thus defied,   68
I thank thee for myself.

Cym.   Thou art welcome, Caius.
Thy Cæsar knighted me; my youth I spent
Much under him; of him I gather'd honour;

---

48 injurious: *insolent*
51 against all colour: *with no pretence of right*
56 whose use: *the operation of which*   57 franchise: *free exercise*

Which he to seek of me again, perforce,   72
Behoves me keep at utterance. I am perfect
That the Pannonians and Dalmatians for
Their liberties are now in arms; a precedent
Which not to read would show the Britons cold: 76
So Cæsar shall not find them.

    Luc.   Let proof speak.

    Clo. His majesty bids you welcome. Make
pastime with us a day or two, or longer; if you
seek us afterwards in other terms, you shall find 80
us in our salt-water girdle; if you beat us out of
it, it is yours; if you fall in the adventure, our
crows shall fare the better for you; and there's
an end.   84

    Luc. So, sir.

    Cym. I know your master's pleasure and he mine:
All the remain is 'Welcome!'   *Exeunt.*

Scene Two

[*The Same*]

Enter Pisanio, reading of a letter.

    Pis. How! of adultery! Wherefore write you not
What monster's her accuser? Leonatus!
O master! what a strange infection
Is fall'n into thy ear! What false Italian—   4
As poisonous-tongued as handed—hath prevail'd
On thy too ready hearing? Disloyal! No:
She's punish'd for her truth, and undergoes,
More goddess-like than wife-like, such assaults   8

72 he to seek: *his seeking*
73 keep at utterance: *vindicate*   perfect: *well-assured*
77 proof speak: *trial show*   87 remain: *rest*

As would take in some virtue. O my master!
Thy mind to her is now as low as were
Thy fortunes. How! that I should murder her?
Upon the love and truth and vows which I   1
Have made to thy command? I, her? her blood?
If it be so to do good service, never
Let me be counted serviceable. How look I,
That I should seem to lack humanity   1
So much as this fact comes to? [*Reads.*] 'Do 't: th
    letter
That I have sent her by her own command
Shall give thee opportunity':—O damn'd paper!
Black as the ink that's on thee. Senseless bauble,   2
Art thou a feodary for this act, and look'st
So virgin-like without? Lo! here she comes.
I am ignorant in what I am commanded.

Enter Imogen.

   Imo. How now, Pisanio!   2
   Pis. Madam, here is a letter from my lord.
   Imo. Who? thy lord? that is my lord, Leonatus.
O! learn'd indeed were that astronomer
That knew the stars as I his characters;   2
He'd lay the future open. You good gods,
Let what is here contain'd relish of love,
Of my lord's health, of his content, yet not
That we two are asunder; let that grieve him,—   3
Some griefs are med'cinable; that is one of them,
For it doth physic love,—of his content,
All but in that! Good wax, thy leave. Bless'd be

---

9 take in: *subdue*   10 to: *in comparison with*
17 fact: *crime*   21 feodary: *accomplic*
23 I am ignorant: *i.e. I shall appear to be ignorant*
27 astronomer: *astrologer*   28 characters: *handwritin*
36 relish: *have a taste*   34 For . . . love; *cf. n*

You bees that make these locks of counsel! Lovers   36
And men in dangerous bonds pray not alike;
Though forfeiters you cast in prison, yet
You clasp young Cupid's tables.   Good news, gods!
[*Reads.*] 'Justice, and your father's wrath, should 40
 he take me in his dominion, could not be so cruel
 to me, as you, O the dearest of creatures, would
 even renew me with your eyes.   Take notice that
 I am in Cambria, at Milford-Haven; what 44
 your own love will out of this advise you, fol-
 low.   So, he wishes you all happiness, that re-
 mains loyal to his vow, and your, increasing in
 love,   Leonatus Posthumus.' 48
O! for a horse with wings!   Hearest thou, Pisanio?
He is at Milford-Haven; read, and tell me
How far 'tis thither.   If one of mean affairs
May plod it in a week, why may not I   52
Glide thither in a day?   Then, true Pisanio,—
Who long'st, like me, to see thy lord; who long'st,—
O! let me 'bate,—but not like me; yet long'st,
But in a fainter kind:—O! not like me,   56
For mine's beyond beyond; say, and speak thick,—
Love's counsellor should fill the bores of hearing,
To the smothering of the sense,—how far it is
To this same blessed Milford; and, by the way, 60
Tell me how Wales was made so happy as
T' inherit such a haven; but, first, of all,
How we may steal from hence, and, for the gap
That we shall make in time, from our hence-going 64
And our return, to excuse; but first, how get hence.
Why should excuse be born or ere begot?

36, 37 Lovers . . . alike; *cf. n.*
39 Cupid's tables: *love-letters*   42, 43 as you . . . eyes; *cf. n.*
51 of mean affairs: *on ordinary business*
55 'bate: *abate, qualify.*   57 thick: *fast*
62 inherit: *possess*   66 *Cf. n.*

We'll talk of that hereafter.   Prithee, speak,
How many score of miles may we well ride   68
'Twixt hour and hour?

   Pis.   One score 'twixt sun and sun,
Madam, 's enough for you, and too much too.

   Imo. Why, one that rode to 's execution, man,
Could never go so slow: I have heard of riding
      wagers,   72
Where horses have been nimbler than the sands
That run i' the clock's behalf.   But this is foolery;
Go bid my woman feign a sickness; say
She'll home to her father; and provide me presently 76
A riding-suit, no costlier than would fit
A franklin's housewife.

   Pis.   Madam, you're best consider.

   Imo. I see before me, man; nor here, nor here,
Nor what ensues, but have a fog in them,   80
That I cannot look through.   Away, I prithee;
Do as I bid thee.   There's no more to say;
Accessible is none but Milford way.   *Exeunt.*

Scene Three

[Wales.   A mountainous Country with a Cave]

*Enter [from the Cave] Belarius, Guiderius, and
      Arviragus.*

   Bel. A goodly day not to keep house, with such
Whose roof's as low as ours!   Stoop, boys; this gate
Instructs you how to adore the heavens, and bows you
To a morning's holy office; the gates of monarchs   4

73, 74 sands . . . behalf; *cf. n.*
78 franklin's: *freeholder's*   you're best: *it were best for you*
79-81 I see . . . through; *cf. n.*   1 keep house: *stay in the house*

Are arch'd so high that giants may jet through
And keep their impious turbans on, without
Good morrow to the sun.   Hail, thou fair heaven!
We house i' the rock, yet use thee not so hardly   8
As prouder livers do.
    Gui.   Hail, heaven!
    Arv.   Hail, heaven!
    Bel. Now for our mountain sport.   Up to yond hill;
Your legs are young; I'll tread these flats.   Consider,
When you above perceive me like a crow,   12
That it is place which lessens and sets off;
And you may then revolve what tales I have told you
Of courts, of princes, of the tricks in war;
This service is not service, so being done;   16
But being so, allow'd: to apprehend thus
Draws us a profit from all things we see,
And often, to our comfort, shall we find
The sharded beetle in a safer hold   20
Than is the full-wing'd eagle.   O! this life
Is nobler than attending for a check,
Richer than doing nothing for a bribe,
Prouder than rustling in unpaid-for silk;   24
Such gain the cap of him that makes 'em fine,
Yet keeps his book uncross'd; no life to ours.
    Gui. Out of your proof you speak; we, poor un-
        fledg'd,
Have never wing'd from view o' the nest, nor know
    not   28
What air 's from home.   Haply this life is best,
If quiet life be best; sweeter to you
That have a sharper known, well corresponding

5 jet: *strut*   16, 17 This service . . . allow'd; *cf. n.*
17 apprehend: *understand*
20 sharded: *with imperfect wings*   hold: *place*
22 attending: *doing service*   check: *rebuke*
25, 26 *Cf. n.*
                                 29 Haply: *perhaps*

With your stiff age; but unto us it is   32
A cell of ignorance, travelling a-bed,
A prison for a debtor that not dares
To stride a limit.
    Arv.   What should we speak of
When we are old as you? when we shall hear   36
The rain and wind beat dark December, how
In this our pinching cave shall we discourse
The freezing hours away? We have seen nothing;
We are beastly, subtle as the fox for prey,   40
Like warlike as the wolf for what we eat;
Our valour is to chase what flies; our cage
We make a choir, as doth the prison'd bird,
And sing our bondage freely.
    Bel.   How you speak!   44
Did you but know the city's usuries
And felt them knowingly; the art o' the court,
As hard to leave as keep, whose top to climb
Is certain falling, or so slippery that   48
The fear's as bad as falling; the toil of the war,
A pain that only seems to seek out danger
I' the name of fame and honour; which dies i' the
    search,
And hath as oft a slanderous epitaph   52
As record of fair act; nay, many times,
Doth ill deserve by doing well; what's worse,
Must curtsy at the censure: O boys! this story
The world may read in me; my body's mark'd   56
With Roman swords, and my report was once
First with the best of note; Cymbeline lov'd me,
And when a soldier was the theme, my name

35 stride a limit: *pass a bound*   38 pinching: *cold*
40 beastly: *like mere beasts*   41 Like. *as*
51 which . . . search; *cf. n.*   57 report: *reputation*
58 with . . . note: *among those of highest fame*

Was not far off; then was I as a tree   60
Whose boughs did bend with fruit, but, in one night,
A storm or robbery, call it what you will,
Shook down my mellow hangings, nay, my leaves,
And left me bare to weather.
 Gui.   Uncertain favour! 64
 Bel. My fault being nothing,—as I have told you
  oft,—
But that two villains, whose false oaths prevail'd
Before my perfect honour, swore to Cymbeline
I was confederate with the Romans; so   68
Follow'd my banishment, and this twenty years
This rock and these demesnes have been my world,
Where I have liv'd at honest freedom, paid
More pious debts to heaven than in all   72
The fore-end of my time. But, up to the mountains!
This is not hunter's language. He that strikes
The venison first shall be the lord o' the feast;
To him the other two shall minister;   76
And we will fear no poison which attends
In place of greater state. I'll meet you in the valleys.
   Exeunt [Guiderius and Arviragus].
How hard it is to hide the sparks of nature!
These boys know little they are sons to the king;   80
Nor Cymbeline dreams that they are alive.
They think they are mine; and, though train'd up thus
  meanly
I' the cave wherein they bow, their thoughts do hit
The roofs of palaces, and nature prompts them   84
In simple and low things to prince it much
Beyond the trick of others. This Polydore,
The heir of Cymbeline and Britain, who
The king his father call'd Guiderius,—Jove!   88

63 hangings: *fruits*   64 weather: *storms*
73 fore-end: *early part*

When on my three-foot stool I sit and tell
The warlike feats I have done, his spirits fly out
Into my story: say, 'Thus mine enemy fell,
And thus I set my foot on 's neck;' even then   92
The princely blood flows in his cheek, he sweats,
Strains his young nerves, and puts himself in posture
That acts my words.   The younger brother, Cadwal,—
Once Arviragus,—in as like a figure,   96
Strikes life into my speech and shows much more
His own conceiving.   Hark! the game is rous'd.
O Cymbeline! heaven and my conscience knows
Thou didst unjustly banish me; whereon,   100
At three and two years old, I stole these babes,
Thinking to bar thee of succession, as
Thou reft'st me of my lands.   Euriphile,
Thou wast their nurse; they took thee for their
          mother,   104
And every day do honour to her grave:
Myself, Belarius, that am Morgan call'd,
They take for natural father.   The game is up.

Exit.

Scene Four

[*Near Milford-Haven*]

Enter Pisanio and Imogen.

Imo. Thou told'st me, when we came from horse,
          the place
Was near at hand: ne'er long'd my mother so
To see me first, as I have now.   Pisanio! man!
Where is Posthumus?   What is in thy mind,   4
That makes thee stare thus?   Wherefore breaks that
          sigh

96-98 in as like . . . conceiving; *cf. n.*

From the inward of thee? One, but painted thus,
Would be interpreted a thing perplex'd
Beyond self-explication; put thyself   8
Into a haviour of less fear, ere wildness
Vanquish my staider senses. What's the matter?
Why tender'st thou that paper to me with
A look untender? If 't be summer news,   12
Smile to 't before; if winterly, thou need'st
But keep that count'nance still. My husband's hand!
That drug-damn'd Italy hath out-craftied him,
And he's at some hard point. Speak, man; thy
    tongue   16
May take off some extremity, which to read
Would be even mortal to me.
   Pis.   Please you, read;
And you shall find me, wretched man, a thing
The most disdain'd of fortune.   20
   Imo. [*Reads.*] 'Thy mistress, Pisanio, hath
played the strumpet in my bed; the testimonies
whereof lie bleeding in me. I speak not out of
weak surmises, but from proof as strong as my 24
grief and as certain as I expect my revenge. That
part thou, Pisanio, must act for me, if thy faith
be not tainted with the breach of hers. Let
thine own hands take away her life; I shall 28
give thee opportunity at Milford-Haven; she
hath my letter for the purpose; where, if thou
fear to strike, and to make me certain it is
done, thou art the pandar to her dishonour and 32
equally to me disloyal.'

9 haviour: *bearing*   wildness: *madness*
12 summer: *i.e. pleasant*
15 drug-damn'd: *detestable for its drugs*   out-craftied: *outwitted*
     by craft
16 point: *predicament*   17 extremity: *extreme rigor*

Pis. What shall I need to draw my sword? the paper
Hath cut her throat already. No, 'tis slander,
Whose edge is sharper than the sword, whose tongue 36
Outvenoms all the worms of Nile, whose breath
Rides on the posting winds and doth belie
All corners of the world; kings, queens, and states,
Maids, matrons, nay, the secrets of the grave   40
This viperous slander enters. What cheer, madam?
    Imo. False to his bed! What is it to be false?
To lie in watch there and to think on him?
To weep 'twixt clock and clock? if sleep charge
        nature,   44
To break it with a fearful dream of him,
And cry myself awake? that's false to 's bed, is it?
    Pis. Alas! good lady.
    Imo. I false! Thy conscience witness! Iachimo, 48
Thou didst accuse him of incontinency;
Thou then look'dst like a villain; now methinks
Thy favour's good enough. Some jay of Italy,
Whose mother was her painting, hath betray'd him: 52
Poor I am stale, a garment out of fashion,
And, for I am richer than to hang by the walls,
I must be ripp'd; to pieces with me! O!
Men's vows are women's traitors! All good
        seeming,   56
By thy revolt, O husband! shall be thought
Put on for villainy; not born where 't grows,
But worn a bait for ladies.
    Pis.   Good madam, hear me.

34 What: *why*   37 worms: *serpents*
38 posting: *speeding*   41 What cheer: *how do you feel?*
43 in watch: *awake*   44 charge: *seize*
51 favour: *appearance*   jay: *showy, light woman*
52 Whose mother . . . painting; *cf. n.*
54 by the walls: *in clothes presses*
                                        56 seeming: *appearance*

Imo. True honest men, being heard like false
   Æneas,   60
Were in his time thought false, and Sinon's weeping
Did scandal many a holy tear, took pity
From most true wretchedness; so thou, Posthumus,
Wilt lay the leaven on all proper men;   64
Goodly and gallant shall be false and perjur'd
From thy great fail. Come, fellow, be thou honest;
Do thou thy master's bidding. When thou seest him,
A little witness my obedience; look!   68
I draw the sword myself; take it, and hit
The innocent mansion of my love, my heart.
Fear not, 'tis empty of all things but grief;
Thy master is not there, who was indeed   72
The riches of it: do his bidding; strike.
Thou mayst be valiant in a better cause,
But now thou seem'st a coward.
Pis.   Hence, vile instrument!
Thou shalt not damn my hand.
Imo.   Why, I must die; 76
And if I do not by thy hand, thou art
No servant of thy master's. Against self-slaughter
There is a prohibition so divine
That cravens my weak hand. Come, here's my heart 80
(Something's afore 't; soft, soft! we'll no defence)
                         [*Taking out letters.*]
Obedient as the scabbard. What is here?
The scriptures of the loyal Leonatus
All turn'd to heresy! Away, away!   84
Corrupters of my faith; you shall no more
Be stomachers to my heart. Thus may poor fools

60, 61 Æneas, Sinon; *cf. n.*   64 proper: *honest*
68 witness: *bear witness to*
80 That cravens: *that it makes cowardly*
82 Obedient: *receptive to the sword*
83 scriptures; *cf. n.*   86 stomachers; *cf. n.*

Believe false teachers; though those that are betrayed
Do feel the treason sharply, yet the traitor   88
Stands in worse case of woe.
And thou, Posthumus, thou that didst set up
My disobedience 'gainst the king my father.
And make me put into contempt the suits   92
Of princely fellows, shalt hereafter find
It is no act of common passage, but
A strain of rareness; and I grieve myself
To think, when thou shalt be disedg'd by her   96
That now thou tir'st on, how thy memory
Will then be pang'd by me.   Prithee, dispatch;
The lamb entreats the butcher; where's thy knife?
Thou art too slow to do thy master's bidding,   100
When I desire it too.
  Pis.   O, gracious lady!
Since I receiv'd command to do this business
I have not slept one wink.
  Imo.   Do 't, and to bed then.
  Pis. I'll wake mine eyeballs first.
  Imo.   Wherefore then 104
Didst undertake it?   Why hast thou abus'd
So many miles with a pretence? this place?
Mine action and thine own? our horses' labour?
The time inviting thee? the perturb'd court,   103
For my being absent?—whereunto I never
Purpose return.—Why hast thou gone so far,
To be unbent when thou hast ta'en thy stand,
The elected deer before thee?
  Pis.   But to win time   112

89 case: *condition*   90 set up: *instigate*
93 fellows: *equals*   94 passage: *occurrence*
95 strain of rareness: *rare impulse*
97 tir'st: *feedest* 98 pang'd: *pained* 96 disedg'd: *satiated*
104 wake: *torture by watching or waking* dispatch: *make haste*
111 unbent: *unprepared, bow unbent* 112 elected: *chosen*

To lose so bad employment, in the which
I have consider'd of a course. Good lady,
Hear me with patience.

  Imo.   Talk thy tongue weary; speak:
I have heard I am a strumpet, and mine ear, 116
Therein false struck, can take no greater wound,
Nor tent to bottom that. But speak.

  Pis.   Then, madam,
I thought you would not back again.

  Imo.   Most like,
Bringing me here to kill me.

  Pis.   Not so, neither; 120
But if I were as wise as honest, then
My purpose would prove well. It cannot be
But that my master is abus'd; some villain,
Some villain, ay, and singular in his art, 124
Hath done you both this cursed injury.

  Imo. Some Roman courtezan.

  Pis.   No, on my life.
I'll give but notice you are dead and send him
Some bloody sign of it; for 'tis commanded 128
I should do so: you shall be miss'd at court,
And that will well confirm it.

  Imo.   Why, good fellow,
What shall I do the while? where bide? how live?
Or in my life what comfort, when I am 132
Dead to my husband?

  Pis.   If you'll back to the court,—

  Imo. No court, no father; nor no more ado
With that harsh, noble, simple nothing!
That Cloten, whose love-suit hath been to me 136
As fearful as a siege.

  Pis.   If not at court,

---

118 tent: *probe*   124 singular: *unmatched*   **135** *Cf. n*

Then not in Britain must you bide.

   Imo.   Where then?

Hath Britain all the sun that shines?   Day, night,

Are they not but in Britain?   I' the world's volume 140

Our Britain seems as of it, but not in 't;

In a great pool a swan's nest: prithee, think

There's livers out of Britain.

   Pis.   I am most glad

You think of other place.   The ambassador,   144

Lucius the Roman, comes to Milford-Haven

To-morrow; now, if you could wear a mind

Dark as your fortune is, and but disguise

That which, t'appear itself, must not yet be   148

But by self-danger, you should tread a course

Pretty, and full of view; yea, haply, near

The residence of Posthumus; so nigh at least

That though his actions were not visible, yet   152

Report should render him hourly to your ear

As truly as he moves.

   Imo.   O! for such means:

Though peril to my modesty, not death on 't,

I would adventure.

   Pis.   Well, then, here's the point: 156

You must forget to be a woman; change

Command into obedience; fear and niceness—

The handmaids of all women, or more truly

Woman it pretty self—into a waggish courage; 160

Ready in gibes, quick-answer'd, saucy, and

As quarrelous as the weasel; nay, you must

140, 141 I' the . . . in 't; *cf. n.*   143 livers: *people living*
146, 147 wear . . . fortune: *make your mind as impenetrable as your
    fortune is dark*
148, 149 That . . . self-danger: *your identity which cannot yet be
    revealed without danger to yourself*
150 Pretty: *fair*   view: *promise*
158 Command: *princely manner of authority*   niceness: *fastidious-
ness*   160 it: *its*   waggish: *pert*

Forget that rarest treasure of your cheek,
Exposing it—but, O! the harder heart,   164
Alack! no remedy—to the greedy touch
Of common-kissing Titan, and forget
Your laboursome and dainty trims, wherein
You made great Juno angry.
   Imo.   Nay, be brief: 168
I see into thy end, and am almost
A man already.
   Pis.   First, make yourself but like one.
Forethinking this, I have already fit—
'Tis in my cloak-bag—doublet, hat, hose, all   172
That answer to them; would you in their serving,
And with what imitation you can borrow
From youth of such a season, 'fore noble Lucius
Present yourself, desire his service, tell him   176
Wherein you are happy,—which will make him know,
If that his head have ear in music,—doubtless
With joy he will embrace you, for he's honourable,
And, doubling that, most holy. Your means abroad, 180
You have me, rich; and I will never fail
Beginning nor supplyment.
   Imo.   Thou art all the comfort
The gods will diet me with. Prithee, away;
There's more to be consider'd, but we'll even   184
All that good time will give us; this attempt
I'm soldier to, and will abide it with
A prince's courage. Away, I prithee.

164 harder: *too hard*
166 common-kissing Titan: *the sun, who kisses everyone*
167 laboursome: *elaborate*   trims: *apparel*
171 Forethinking: *anticipating*   fit: *prepared*
173 in their serving: *with their help*
177 happy: *skillful*   177, 178 which . . . music; *cf. n.*
180 doubling: *in addition to*   Your means abroad: *as for the ex-*
    penses of your journey   183 diet: *feed*
184 even: *act up to, keep pace with*
186 soldier to: *enlisted to*   abide: *encounter*

Pis. Well, madam, we must take a short farewell, 188
Lest, being miss'd, I be suspected of
Your carriage from the court.   My noble mistress,
Here is a box, I had it from the queen,
What's in 't is precious; if you are sick at sea,   192
Or stomach-qualm'd at land, a dram of this
Will drive away distemper.   To some shade,
And fit you to your manhood.   May the gods
Direct you to the best!
     Imo.   Amen.   I thank thee.   *Exeunt.*

Scene Five

[Cymbeline's Palace]

*Enter Cymbeline, Queen, Cloten, Lucius, Lords [and
Attendants].*

     Cym. Thus far; and so farewell.
     Luc.   Thanks, royal sir.
My emperor hath wrote, I must from hence;
And am right sorry that I must report ye
My master's enemy.
     Cym.   Our subjects, sir,   4
Will not endure his yoke; and for ourself
To show less sovereignty than they, must needs
Appear unkinglike.
     Luc.   So, sir: I desire of you
A conduct over land to Milford-Haven.   8
Madam, all joy befall your Grace, and you.
     Cym. My lords, you are appointed for that office;
The due of honour in no point omit.
So, farewell, noble Lucius.

190 carriage: *abduction*
194 distemper: *illness*   To some shade: *withdraw to some secluded*
        place   *place*
                              9 your Grace, and you; *cf. n.*

   Luc.   Your hand, my lord.   12
   Clo. Receive it friendly; but from this time forth
I wear it as your enemy.
   Luc.   Sir, the event
Is yet to name the winner. Fare you well.
   Cym. Leave not the worthy Lucius, good my
     lords,   16
Till he have crossed the Severn. Happiness!
                        Exit Lucius, &c.
   Queen. He goes hence frowning; but it honours us
That we have given him cause.
   Clo.   'Tis all the better;
Your valiant Britons have their wishes in it.   20
   Cym. Lucius hath wrote already to the emperor
How it goes here. It fits us therefore ripely
Our chariots and horsemen be in readiness;
The powers that he already hath in Gallia   24
Will soon be drawn to head, from whence he moves
His war for Britain.
   Queen.   'Tis not sleepy business;
But must be look'd to speedily and strongly.
   Cym. Our expectation that it would be thus   28
Hath made us forward. But, my gentle queen,
Where is our daughter? She hath not appear'd
Before the Roman, nor to us hath tender'd
The duty of the day; she looks us like   32
A thing more made of malice than of duty:
We have noted it. Call her before us, for
We have been too slight in sufferance.

                   [Exit an Attendant.]
   Queen.   Royal sir.
Since the exile of Posthumus, most retir'd   36

14 event: *outcome*   22 fits: *behooves*   ripely: *promptly*
25 drawn to head: *gathered into a military force*
35 slight in sufferance: *careless in forbearance*

Hath her life been; the cure whereof, my lord,
'Tis time must do.   Beseech your majesty,
Forbear sharp speeches to her; she's a lady
So tender of rebukes that words are strokes,   40
And strokes death to her.

Enter a Messenger.

   Cym.   Where is she, sir?   How
Can her contempt be answer'd?
   Mes.   Please you, sir,
Her chambers are all lock'd, and there's no answer
That will be given to the loudest of noise we make.   44
   Queen. My lord, when last I went to visit her,
She pray'd me to excuse her keeping close,
Whereto constrain'd by her infirmity,
She should that duty leave unpaid to you,   48
Which daily she was bound to proffer; this
She wish'd me to make known, but our great court
Made me to blame in memory.
   Cym.   Her doors lock'd!
Not seen of late!   Grant, heavens, that which I fear 52
Prove false!   *Exit.*
   Queen.   Son, I say, follow the king.
   Clo. That man of hers, Pisario, her old servant,
I have not seen these two days.
   Queen.   Go, look after.
                          Exit [*Cloten*].
Pisanio, thou that stand'st so for Posthumus!   56
He hath a drug of mine; I pray his absence
Proceed by swallowing that, for he believes
It is a thing most precious.   But for her,
Where is she gone?   Haply, despair hath seiz'd her, 60
Or, wing'd with fervour of her love, she's flown
To her desir'd Posthumus.   Gone she is

To death or to dishonour, and my end
Can make good use of either; she being down,   64
I have the placing of the British crown.

Enter Cloten.

How now, my son!
   Clo.   'Tis certain she is fled.
Go in and cheer the king; he rages, none
Dare come about him.
   Queen.   [*Aside.*] All the better; may 68
This night forestall him of the coming day!
                    Exit Qu[een].

   Clo. I love and hate her; for she's fair and royal,
And that she hath all courtly parts more exquisite
Than lady, ladies, woman; from every one   72
The best she hath, and she, of all compounded,
Outsells them all.   I love her therefore; but
Disdaining me and throwing favours on
The low Posthumus slanders so her judgment   76
That what's else rare is chok'd, and in that point
I will conclude to hate her, nay, indeed,
To be reveng'd upon her.   For, when fools
Shall—

Enter Pisanio.

     Who is here?   What! are you packing, sirrah? 80
Come hither.   Ah! you precious pandar.   Villain,
Where is thy lady?   In a word; or else
Thou art straightway with the fiends.
   Pis.   O! good my lord.
   Clo. Where is thy lady? or, by Jupiter   84
I will not ask again.   Close villain,
I'll have this secret from thy heart, or rip
Thy heart to find it.   Is she with Posthumus?

69 forestall him of: *prevent his living to see*
80 packing: *departing*   85 Close: *secretive*

From whose so many weights of baseness cannot   88
A dram of worth be drawn.

   Pis.   Alas! my lord,
How can she be with him? When was she miss'd?
He is in Rome.

   Clo.   Where is she, sir? Come nearer,
No further halting; satisfy me home   92
What is become of her?

   Pis. O! my all-worthy lord.

   Clo.   All-worthy villain!
Discover where thy mistress is at once,
At the next word; no more of 'worthy lord!'   96
Speak, or thy silence on the instant is
Thy condemnation and thy death.

   Pis.   Then, sir,
This paper is the history of my knowledge
Touching her flight.   [*Presenting a letter.*]

   Clo.   Let's see 't. I will pursue her 100
Even to Augustus' throne.

   Pis.   [*Aside.*] Or this, or perish.
She's far enough; and what he learns by this
May prove his travel, not her danger.

   Clo.   Hum!

   Pis. [*Aside.*] I'll write to my lord she's dead. O
     Imogen!   104
Safe mayst thou wander, safe return again!

   Clo. Sirrah, is this letter true?

   Pis. Sir, as I think.

   Clo. It is Posthumus' hand; I know 't. Sir- 108
rah, if thou wouldst not be a villain, but do me
true service, undergo those employments wherein
I should have cause to use thee with a serious

industry, that is, what villainy soe'er I bid thee 112
do, to perform it directly and truly, I would
think thee an honest man; thou shouldst neither
want my means for thy relief nor my voice for
thy preferment.   116

Pis. Well, my good lord.

Clo. Wilt thou serve me? For since patiently
and constantly thou hast stuck to the bare fortune of that beggar Posthumus, thou canst not, 120
in the course of gratitude, but be a diligent fol-
lower of mine. Wilt thou serve me?

Pis. Sir, I will.

Clo. Give me thy hand; here's my purse. 124
Hast any of thy late master's garments in thy
possession?

Pis. I have, my lord, at my lodging the same
suit he wore when he took leave of my lady and 128
mistress.

Clo. The first service thou dost me, fetch that
suit hither: let it be thy first service; go.

Pis. I shall, my lord.   *Exit.* 132

Clo. Meet thee at Milford-Haven!—I forgot
to ask him one thing; I'll remember 't anon—
even there, thou villain Posthumus, will I kill
thee. I would these garments were come. She 136
said upon a time,—the bitterness of it I now
belch from my heart,—that she held the very
garment of Posthumus in more respect than my
noble and natural person, together with the 140
adornment of my qualities. With that suit upon
my back will I ravish her: first kill him, and in
her eyes; there shall she see my valour, which
will then be a torment to her contempt. He on 144
the ground, my speech of insultment ended on

his dead body, and when my lust hath dined,
—which, as I say, to vex her, I will execute in
the clothes that she so praised,—to the court I'll 148
knock her back, foot her home again. She hath
despised me rejoicingly, and I'll be merry in my
revenge.

Enter Pisanio [with the clothes].

Be those the garments?　　　　　　　　　　152
Pis. Ay, my noble lord.
Clo. How long is 't since she went to Milford-
　　Haven?
Pis. She can scarce be there yet.
　Clo. Bring this apparel to my chamber; that 156
is the second thing that I have commanded thee;
the third is, that thou wilt be a voluntary mute
to my design. Be but duteous, and true prefer-
ment shall tender itself to thee. My revenge is 160
now at Milford; would I had wings to follow it.
Come, and be true.　　　　　　　　　　*Exit.*
　Pis. Thou bidd'st me to my loss; for true to thee
Were to prove false, which I will never be, 164
To him that is most true. To Milford go,
And find not her whom thou pursu'st. Flow, flow,
You heavenly blessings, on her! This fool's speed
Be cross'd with slowness; labour be his meed! *Exit.*

158 a voluntary mute to : *voluntarily silent respecting*
168 labour be his meed: *his pains be his reward*

Scene Six

[Wales.   Before the Cave of Belarius]

Enter Imogen [in boy's clothes].

Imo. I see a man's life is a tedious one;
I have tir'd myself, and for two nights together
Have made the ground my bed; I should be sick
But that my resolution helps me.   Milford,   4
When from the mountain-top Pisanio show'd thee,
Thou wast within a ken.   O Jove! I think
Foundations fly the wretched; such, I mean,
Where they should be reliev'd.   Two beggars told me 8
I could not miss my way; will poor folks lie,
That have afflictions on them, knowing 'tis
A punishment or trial?   Yes; no wonder,
When rich ones scarce tell true.   To lapse in fulness 12
Is sorer than to lie for need, and falsehood
Is worse in kings than beggars.   My dear lord!
Thou art one o' the false ones.   Now I think on thee,
My hunger's gone, but even before I was   16
At point to sink for food.   But what is this?
Here is a path to 't; 'tis some savage hold;
I were best not call, I dare not call, yet famine,
Ere clean it o'erthrow nature, makes it valiant.   20
Plenty and peace breeds cowards, hardness ever
Of hardiness is mother.   Ho! Who's here?
If anything that's civil, speak; if savage,
Take or lend.   Ho! No answer?   Then I'll enter.   24
Best draw my sword; and if mine enemy

6 within a ken: *in sight*
12 lapse: *fall into sin*   fulness: *prosperity*
13 sorer: *more grievous*
20 clean: *entirely*
22 hardiness: *courage*
24 Take or lend; *cf. n.*

7 Foundations; *cf. n.*

16 even: *just*
21 hardness: *difficulty*
23 civil: *civilized*

But fear the sword like me, he'll scarcely look on 't.
Such a foe, good heavens!   *Exit* [*to the cave*].

Enter Belarius, Guiderius, and Arviragus.

  Bel. You, Polydore, have prov'd best woodman,
      and   28
Are master of the feast; Cadwal and I
Will play the cook and servant, 'tis our match;
The sweat of industry would dry and die
But for the end it works to.   Come; our stomachs 32
Will make what's homely savoury; weariness
Can snore upon the flint when resty sloth
Finds the down pillow hard.   Now, peace be here,
Poor house, that keep'st thyself!
  Gui.   I am throughly weary. 36
  Arv. I am weak with toil, yet strong in appetite.
  Gui. There is cold meat i' the cave; we'll browse on
      that,
Whilst what we have kill'd be cook'd.
  Bel. [*Looking into the cave.*] Stay; come not in;
But that it eats our victuals, I should think   40
Here were a fairy.
  Gui.   What's the matter, sir?
  Bel. By Jupiter, an angel! or, if not,
An earthly paragon!   Behold diviness
No elder than a boy!   44

Enter Imogen.

  Imo. Good masters, harm me not:
Before I enter'd here, I call'd; and thought
To have begg'd or bought what I have took.   Good
      troth,

27 Such a foe; *cf. n.*   28 woodman: *huntsman*
30 match: *compact*
34 snore upon the flint: *sleep on a bed of stones*   resty: *sluggish*

I have stol'n nought, nor would not, though I had
    found   48
Gold strew'd i' the floor. Here's money for my meat;
I would have left it on the board so soon
As I had made my meal, and parted
With prayers for the provider.

    Gui.   Money, youth?   52

    Arv. All gold and silver rather turn to dirt!
As 'tis no better reckon'd but of those
Who worship dirty gods.

    Imo.   I see you're angry.

Know, if you kill me for my fault, I should   56
Have died had I not made it.

    Bel.   Whither bound?

    Imo. To Milford-Haven.

    Bel. What's your name?

    Imo. Fidele, sir. I have a kinsman who   60
Is bound for Italy; he embark'd at Milford:
To whom being going, almost spent with hunger,
I am fall'n in this offence.

    Bel.   Prithee, fair youth,
Think us no churls, nor measure our good minds   64
By this rude place we live in. Well encounter'd!
'Tis almost night; you shall have better cheer
Ere you depart, and thanks to stay and eat it.
Boys, bid him welcome.

    Gui.   Were you a woman, youth, 68
I should woo hard but be your groom. In honesty
I bid for you, as I do buy.

    Arv.   I'll make 't my comfort
He is a man; I'll love him as my brother;
And such a welcome as I'd give to him   72

51 parted: *departed*   64 churls: *boors*
56 cheer: *entertainment*   69, 70 In honesty . . . buy; *cf. n.*

After long absence, such is yours: most welcome!
Be sprightly, for you fall 'mongst friends.
   Imo.   'Mongst friends,
If brothers. [*Aside.*] Would it had been so, that they
Had been my father's sons; then had my prize   76
Been less, and so more equal ballasting
To thee, Posthumus.
   Bel.   He wrings at some distress.
   Gui. Would I could free 't!
   Arv.   Or I, whate'er it be,
What pain it cost, what danger.   Gods!
   Bel.   Hark, boys. 80
                          [*Whispering.*]

   Imo. [*Aside.*] Great men,
That had a court no bigger than this cave,
That did attend themselves and had the virtue
Which their own conscience seal'd them,—laying by 84
That nothing-gift of differing multitudes,—
Could not out-peer these twain.   Pardon me, gods!
I'd change my sex to be companion with them,
Since Leonatus' false.
   Bel.   It shall be so.   88
Boys, we'll go dress our hunt.   Fair youth, come in:
Discourse is heavy, fasting; when we have supp'd,
We'll mannerly demand thee of thy story,
So far as thou wilt speak it.
   Gui.   Pray, draw near.   92
   Arv. The night to the owl and morn to the lark less
     welcome.
   Imo. Thanks, sir.
   Arv.   I pray, draw near.   *Exeunt.*

74 sprightly: *cheerful*   **76** prize: *value, hence importance*
77 ballasting: *weight*   **78** wrings: *writhes*
84, 85 laying by . . . multitudes; *cf. n.*
86 out-peer: *surpass*   **89** hunt: *game*

Scene Seven

[*Rome.   A Public Place*]

Enter two Senators and Tribunes.

1. Sen. This is the tenour of the emperor's **writ:**
That since the common men are now in action
'Gainst the Pannonians and Dalmatians,
And that the legions now in Gallia are   4
Full weak to undertake our wars against
The fall'n-off Britons, that we do incite
The gentry to this business.   He creates
Lucius pro-consul; and to you the tribunes,   8
For this immediate levy, he commends
His absolute commission.   Long live Cæsar!
    1. Tri. Is Lucius general of the forces?
    2. Sen.   **Ay.**
    1. Tri. Remaining now in Gallia?
    1. Sen.   With those legions 12
Which I have spoke of, whereunto your levy
Must be supplyant; the words of your commission
Will tie you to the numbers and the time
Of their dispatch.
    1. Tri.   We will discharge our duty.   16
                                            Exeunt.

6 fall'n-off. *revolted*   9 commends: *delivers*
14 supplyant: *supplementary*

ACT FOURTH

Scene One

[Wales.   The Forest, near the Cave of Belarius]

Enter Cloten.

Clo. I am near to the place where they should
meet, if Pisanio have mapped it truly.   How fit
his garments serve me!   Why should his mistress, who was made by him that made the tailor, 4
not be fit too? the rather,—saving reverence of
the word,—for 'tis said a woman's fitness comes
by fits.   Therein I must play the workman.   I
dare speak it to myself.—for it is not vain-glory 8
for a man and his glass to confer in his own
chamber,—I mean, the lines of my body are as
well drawn as his; no less young, more strong,
not beneath him in fortunes, beyond him in the 12
advantage of the time, above him in birth, alike
conversant in general services, and more remark-
able in single oppositions; yet this imperceiverant thing loves him in my despite.   What 16
mortality is!   Posthumus, thy head, which now
is growing upon thy shoulders, shall within this
hour be off, thy mistress enforced, thy garments
cut to pieces before thy face; and all this done, 20
spurn her home to her father, who may happily
be a little angry for my so rough usage, but my
mother, having power of his testiness, shall turn

2 fit: *fittingly*   5 saving reverence: *begging pardon*
6 fitness: *inclination (used in an objectionable sense)*
13 time: *present circumstances*   14 general services: *public affairs*
15 oppositions: *combats*   imperceiverant: *undiscerning*
19 enforced: *ravished*   21 spurn: *kick*   happily: *perchance*
23 power of: *control over*

all into my commendations. My horse is tied 24
up safe; out, sword, and to a sore purpose!
Fortune, put them into my hand! This is the
very description of their meeting place; and the
fellow dares not deceive me.   *Exit.*

Scene Two

[Before the Cave of Belarius]

*Enter [from the Cave] Belarius, Guiderius, Arviragus,
and Imogen.*

Bel. [*To Imogen.*] You are not well; remain here
   in the cave;
We'll come to you after hunting.
  Arv.   [*To Imogen.*] Brother, stay here;
Are we not brothers?
  Imo.   So man and man should be,
But clay and clay differs in dignity,   4
Whose dust is both alike. I am very sick.
  Gui. Go you to hunting; I'll abide with him.
  Imo. So sick I am not, yet I am not well;
But not so citizen a wanton as   8
To seem to die ere sick. So please you, leave me;
Stick to your journal course; the breach of custom
Is breach of all. I am ill; but your being by me
Cannot amend me; society is no comfort   12
To one not sociable. I am not very sick,
Since I can reason of it; pray you, trust me here,
I'll rob none but myself, and let me die,
Stealing so poorly.
  Gui.   I love thee; I have spoke it;   16

8 citizen . . . wanton: *city-bred spoilt child, "tenderfoot"*
10 journal: *daily*   14 reason: *talk*

How much the quantity, the weight as much,
As I do love my father.

   Bel.   What! how! how!

   Arv. If it be sin to say so, sir, I yoke me
In my good brother's fault: I know not why   20
I love this youth; and I have heard you say,
Love's reason's without reason: the bier at door,
And a demand who is 't shall die, I'd say
'My father, not this youth.'

   Bel. [*Aside.*]   O noble strain!   24
O worthiness of nature! breed of greatness!
Cowards father cowards, and base things sire base:
Nature hath meal and bran, contempt and grace.
I'm not their father; yet who this should be   28
Doth miracle itself, lov'd before me.
'Tis the ninth hour o' the morn.

   Arv.   Brother, farewell.

   Imo. I wish ye sport.

   Arv.   You health. So please you, sir.

   Imo. [*Aside.*] These are kind creatures. Gods, what
     lies I have heard!   32
Our courtiers say all's savage but at court:
Experience, O, thou disprov'st report!
The imperious seas breed monsters, for the dish
Poor tributary rivers as sweet fish.   36
I am sick still, heart-sick. Pisanio,
I'll now taste of thy drug.   [*Swallows some.*]

   Gui.   I could not stir him;
He said he was gentle, but unfortunate;
Dishonestly afflicted, but yet honest.   40

   Arv. Thus did he answer me; yet said hereafter
I might know more.

Bel.   To the field, to the field!
[*To Imogen.*] We'll leave you for this time; go in and
  rest.
Arv. We'll not be long away.
Bel.   Pray, be not sick, 44
For you must be our housewife.
Imo.   Well or ill,
I am bound to you.   *Exit.*
Bel.   And shalt be ever.
This youth, howe'er distress'd, appears he hath had
Good ancestors.
Arv.   How angel-like he sings!   48
Gui. But his neat cookery! he cut our roots
In characters,
And sauc'd our broths as Juno had been sick
And he her dieter.
Arv.   Nobly he yokes
A smiling with a sigh, as if the sigh   52
Was that it was, for not being such a smile;
The smile mocking the sigh, that it would fly
From so divine a temple, to commix
With winds that sailors rail at.
Gui.   I do note   56
That grief and patience, rooted in him both,
Mingle their spurs together.
Arv.   Grow, patience!
And let the stinking-elder, grief, untwine
His perishing root with the increasing vine!   60
  Bel. It is great morning. Come, away!—Who's
  there?

Enter Cloten.

---

50 characters: *letters*   58 spurs: *roots*
49 stinking-elder; *cf. n.*
50 with . . . vine: *i.e. as the vine, patience, grows*
51 great morning: *broad day*

Clo. I cannot find those runagates; that villain
Hath mock'd me.   I am faint.

Bel.   'Those runagates!'
Means he not us?   I partly know him; 'tis   64
Cloten, the son o' the queen.   I fear some ambush.
I saw him not these many years, and yet
I know 'tis he.   We are held as outlaws: hence!

Gui. He is but one.   You and my brother search 68
What companies are near; pray you, away;
Let me alone with him.

                    [*Exeunt Belarius and Arviragus.*]
Clo.   Soft!   What are you
That fly me thus? some villain mountainers?
I have heard of such.   What slave art thou?

Gui.   A thing 72
More slavish did I ne'er than answering
A 'slave' without a knock.

Clo.   Thou art a robber,
A law-breaker, a villain.   Yield thee, thief.

Gui. To who? to thee?   What art thou?   Have
    not I   76
An arm as big as thine? a heart as big?
Thy words, I grant, are bigger, for I wear not
My dagger in my mouth.   Say what thou art,
Why I should yield to thee?

Clo.   Thou villain base,   80
Know'st me not by my clothes?

Gui.   No, nor thy tailor, rascal,
Who is thy grandfather: he made those clothes,
Which, as it seems, make thee.

Clo.   Thou precious varlet,
My tailor made them not.

Gui.   Hence then, and thank 84

74 A 'slave': *i.e. the epithet 'slave'*   81 my clothes; *cf. n.*
83 precious: *arrant*   varlet: *knave*

The man that gave them thee.   Thou art some fool;
am loath to beat thee.
 Clo.   Thou injurious thief,
Hear but my name, and tremble.
 Gui.   What's thy name?
 Clo. Cloten, thou villain.   88
 Gui. Cloten, thou double villain, be thy name,
cannot tremble at it; were it Toad, or Adder, Spider,
I would move me sooner.
 Clo.   To thy further fear,
Nay, to thy mere confusion, thou shalt know 92
am son to the queen.
 Gui.   I'm sorry for 't, not seeming
so worthy as thy birth.
 Clo.   Art not afeard?
 Gui. Those that I reverence those I fear, the wise;
t fools I laugh, not fear them.
 Clo.   Die the death: 96
Then I have slain thee with my proper hand,
Ill follow those that even now fled hence,
and on the gates of Lud's town set your heads:
Yield, rustic mountaineer. *Fight and exeunt.* 100

   Enter Belarius and Arviragus.

 Bel. No companies abroad?
 Arv. None in the world.   You did mistake him, sure.
 Bel. I cannot tell; long is it since I saw him,
But time hath nothing blurr'd those lines of favour 104
Which then he wore; the snatches in his voice,
and burst of speaking, were as his.   I am absolute
'Twas very Cloten.
 Arv.   In this place we left them:

mere: *sheer*
 snatches: *sudden checks*   97 proper: *own*
 very Cloten: *Cloten himself* 106 absolute: *certain*

I wish my brother make good time with him,   10
You say he is so fell.

 Bel.   Being scarce made up,
I mean, to man, he had not apprehension
Of roaring terrors; for defect of judgment
Is oft the cause of fear. But see, thy brother.   11

 Enter Guiderius [with Cloten's head].

 Gui. This Cloten was a fool, an empty purse,
There was no money in 't. Not Hercules
Could have knock'd out his brains, for he had none;
Yet I not doing this, the fool had borne   11
My head as I do his.

 Bel.   What hast thou done?

 Gui. I am perfect what: cut off one Cloten's head,
Son to the queen after his own report,
Who call'd me traitor, mountaineer, and swore,   12
With his own single hand he'd take us in,
Displace our heads where—thank the gods!—the
  grow,
And set them on Lud's town.

 Bel.   We are all undone.

 Gui. Why, worthy father, what have we to lose,   1
But that he swore to take, our lives? The law
Protects not us; then why should we be tender
To let an arrogant piece of flesh threat us,
Play judge and executioner all himself,   1
For we do fear the law? What company
Discover you abroad?

 Bel.   No single soul
Can we set eye on; but in all safe reason   1
He must have some attendants. Though his humo

109 fell: *fierce*   109-112 Being scarce . . . fear; *cf.*
129 For: *because*   131 safe: *sou*

Was nothing but mutation, ay, and that
From one bad thing to worse; not frenzy, not
Absolute madness could so far have rav'd
To bring him here alone.   Although, perhaps,   136
It may be heard at court that such as we
Cave here, hunt here, are outlaws, and in time
May make some stronger head; the which he hearing,—
As it is like him,—might break out, and swear   140
He'd fetch us in; yet is 't not probable
To come alone, either he so undertaking,
Or they so suffering; then, on good ground we fear,
If we do fear this body hath a tail   144
More perilous than the head.

 Arv.   Let ordinance
Come as the gods foresay it; howsoe'er,
My brother hath done well.

 Bel.   I had no mind
To hunt this day; the boy Fidele's sickness   148
Did make my way long forth.

 Gui.   With his own sword,
Which he did wave against my throat, I have ta'en
His head from him; I'll throw 't into the creek
Behind our rock, and let it to the sea,   152
And tell the fishes he's the queen's son, Cloten:
That's all I reck.   *Exit.*

 Bel.   I fear 'twill be reveng'd.
Would, Polydore, thou hadst not done 't! though valour
Becomes thee well enough.

 Arv.   Would I had done 't,   156
So the revenge alone pursu'd me! Polydore,
I love thee brotherly, but envy much

33 nothing but mutation: *for constant change*
41 fetch us in: *capture us*   145 ordinance: *divine decree*
49 way long forth: *walking forth seem long* 154 reck: *care*

Thou hast robb'd me of this deed; I would revenges,
That possible strength might meet, would seek us
    through   160
And put us to our answer.
    Bel.   Well, 'tis done.—
We'll hunt no more to-day, nor seek for danger
Where there's no profit.   I prithee, to our rock;
You and Fidele play the cooks; I'll stay   164
Till hasty Polydore return, and bring him
To dinner presently.
    Arv.   Poor sick Fidele!
I'll willingly to him; to gain his colour
I'd let a parish of such Clotens blood,   168
And praise myself for charity.   *Exit.*
    Bel.   O thou goddess!
Thou, divine Nature thou, thyself thou blazon'st
In these two princely boys.   They are as gentle
As zephyrs, blowing below the violet,   172
Not wagging his sweet head; and yet as rough,
Their royal blood enchaf'd, as the rud'st wind,
That by the top doth take the mountain pine,
And make him stoop to the vale.   'Tis wonder   176
That an invisible instinct should frame them
To royalty unlearn'd, honour untaught,
Civility not seen from other, valour
That wildly grows in them, but yields a crop   180
As if it had been sow'd!   Yet still it's strange
What Cloten's being here to us portends,
Or what his death will bring us.

Enter Guiderius.

    Gui.   Where's my brother?

159-161 I would . . . answer; *cf. n.*   167 gain: *restore*
174 enchaf'd: *excited*   179 seen from other: *observed in others*
180 wildly: *without cultivation*

I have sent Cloten's clotpoll down the stream,   184
In embassy to his mother; his body's hostage
For his return.   *Solemn music.*
   Bel.   My ingenious instrument!
Hark! Polydore, it sounds; but what occasion
Hath Cadwal now to give it motion? Hark!   188
   Gui. Is he at home?
   Bel.   He went hence even now.
   Gui. What does he mean? since death of my dear'st
    mother
It did not speak before. All solemn things
Should answer solemn accidents. The matter?   192
Triumphs for nothing and lamenting toys
Is jollity for apes and grief for boys.
Is Cadwal mad?

*Enter Arviragus, with Imogen, [as] dead, bearing her
in his arms.*

   Bel.   Look! here he comes,
And brings the dire occasion in his arms   196
Of what we blame him for.
   Arv.   The bird is dead
That we have made so much on. I had rather
Have skipp'd from sixteen years of age to sixty,
To have turn'd my leaping-time into a crutch,   200
Than have seen this.
   Gui.   O, sweetest, fairest lily!
My brother wears thee not the one half so well
As when thou grew'st thyself.
   Bel.   O melancholy!
Who ever yet could sound thy bottom? find   204
The ooze, to show what coast thy sluggish crare

184 clotpoll: *thick head*
192 answer: *correspond to*   accidents: *occurrences*
193 lamenting toys: *lamentation for trifles*   194 apes: *fools*
200 leaping-time: *youth*   205 crare: *small vessel*

Might easiliest harbour in? Thou blessed thing!
Jove knows what man thou mightst have made; but ay!
Thou diedst, a most rare boy, of melancholy.   208
How found you him?

    Arv.   Stark, as you see:
Thus smiling, as some fly had tickled slumber,
Not as death's dart, being laugh'd at; his right cheek
Reposing on a cushion.

    Gui.   Where?

    Arv.   O' the floor,   212
His arms thus leagu'd; I thought he slept, and put
My clouted brogues from off my feet, whose rudeness
Answer'd my steps too loud.

    Gui.   Why, he but sleeps:
If he be gone, he'll make his grave a bed;   216
With female fairies will his tomb be haunted,
And worms will not come to thee.

    Arv.   With fairest flowers,
While summer lasts and I live here, Fidele,
I'll sweeten thy sad grave; thou shalt not lack   220
The flower that's like thy face, pale primrose, nor
The azur'd hare-bell, like thy veins, no, nor
The leaf of eglantine, whom not to slander,
Out-sweeten'd not thy breath: the ruddock would   224
With charitable bill,—O bill sore-shaming
Those rich-left heirs, that let their fathers lie
Without a monument,—bring thee all this;
Yea, and furr'd moss besides, when flowers are
    none,   228
To winter-ground thy corse.

    Gui.   Prithee, have done,
And do not play in wench-like words with that

---

207 ay: *alas*   214 clouted brogues: *heavy shoes studded with hobnails*
224 ruddock: *robin*   229 winter-ground: *cover for the winter*
230 wench-like: *womanish*

Which is so serious.   Let us bury him,
And not protract with admiration what   232
Is now due debt.   To the grave !
 Arv.   Say, where shall's lay him?
 Gui. By good Euriphile, our mother.
 Arv.   Be 't so:
And let us, Polydore, though now our voices   235
Have got the mannish crack, sing him to the ground,
As once to our mother; use like note and words,
Save that Euriphile must be Fidele.
 Gui. Cadwal,
I cannot sing; I'll weep, and word it with thee;   240
For notes of sorrow out of tune are worse
Than priests and fanes that lie.
 Arv.   We'll speak it then.
 Bel. Great griefs, I see, medicine the less, for Cloten
Is quite forgot.   He was a queen's son, boys,   244
And though he came our enemy, remember
He was paid for that; though mean and mighty,
 rotting
Together, have one dust, yet reverence—
That angel of the world—doth make distinction   248
Of place 'tween high and low.   Our foe was princely,
And though you took his life, as being our foe,
Yet bury him as a prince.
 Gui.   Pray you, fetch him hither.
Thersites' body is as good as Ajax'   252
When neither are alive.
 Arv.   If you'll go fetch him,
We'll say our song the whilst.   Brother, begin.
          [Exit Belarius.]

233 shall's: *shall we*
237 to our mother: *i.e. as once we sang our mother*   like: *the same*
242 fanes: *temple oracles*   243 medicine: *cure*
246 paid: *punished*   252 Thersites' . . . Ajax'; *cf. n.*

Gui. Nay, Cadwal, we must lay his head to the east;
My father hath a reason for 't.

Arv.   'Tis true.   256

Gui. Come on then, and remove him.

Arv.   So, begin.

Gui. 'Fear no more the heat o' the sun,
            Nor the furious winter's rages;
        Thou thy worldly task hast done,   260
            Home art gone, and ta'en thy wages;
        Golden lads and girls all must,
            As chimney-sweepers, come to dust.

Arv. 'Fear no more the frown o' the great,   264
            Thou art past the tyrant's stroke:
        Care no more to clothe and eat;
            To thee the reed is as the oak:
        The sceptre, learning, physic, must   268
            All follow this, and come to dust.

Gui. 'Fear no more the lightning-flash,

Arv.   'Nor the all-dreaded thunder-stone;

Gui. 'Fear not slander, censure rash;   272

Arv.   'Thou hast finished joy and moan:

Both. 'All lovers young, all lovers must
            Consign to thee, and come to dust.

Gui. 'No exorciser harm thee!   276

Arv.   'Nor no witchcraft charm thee!

Gui. 'Ghost unlaid forbear thee!

Arv.   'Nothing ill come near thee!

Both. 'Quiet consummation have;   280
            And renowned be thy grave!'

Enter Belarius, with the body of Cloten.

Gui. We have done our obsequies. Come, lay him
down.

271 thunder-stone: *thunderbolt*   275 Consign: *subscribe*
276 exorciser: *conjurer*

Bel. Here's a few flowers, but 'bout midnight, more;
The herbs that have on them cold dew o' the night   284
Are strewings fitt'st for graves.   Upon their faces.
You were as flowers, now wither'd; even so
These herblets shall, which we upon you strew.
Come on, away; apart upon our knees.   288
The ground that gave them first has them again;
Their pleasures here are past, so is their pain.

      Exeunt [Belarius, Guiderius, and Arviragus].
                       Imogen awakes.

  Imo. Yes, sir, to Milford-Haven; which is the way?
I thank you.   By yond bush?   Pray, how far thither?
'Ods pittikins! can it be six mile yet?   293
I have gone all night: Faith, I'll lie down and sleep.
[*Seeing the body of Cloten.*] But, soft! no bedfellow!
    O gods and goddesses!
These flowers are like the pleasures of the world;   296
This bloody man, the care on 't.   I hope I dream;
For so I thought I was a cave-keeper,
And cook to honest creatures; but 'tis not so,
'Twas but a bolt of nothing, shot at nothing,   300
Which the brain makes of fumes.   Our very eyes
Are sometimes like our judgments, blind.   Good faith,
I tremble still with fear; but if there be
Yet left in heaven as small a drop of pity   304
As a wren's eye, fear'd gods, a part of it!
The dream's here still; even when I wake, it is
Without me, as within me; not imagin'd, felt.
A headless man! The garments of Posthumus!   308
I know the shape of 's leg, this is his hand,
His foot Mercurial, his Martial thigh,
The brawns of Hercules, but his Jovial face—

285 Upon . . . faces; *cf. n.*
293 'Ods: *God's*   pittikins: *diminutive form of pity*
301 fumes: *vapors*   310, 311 *Cf. n.*

Murder in heaven? How! 'Tis gone. Pisanio,   312
All curses madded Hecuba gave the Greeks,
And mine to boot, be darted on thee! Thou,
Conspir'd with that irregulous devil, Cloten,
Hast here cut off my lord. To write and read   316
Be henceforth treacherous! Damn'd Pisanio
Hath with his forged letters, damn'd Pisanio,
From this most bravest vessel of the world
Struck the main-top! O Posthumus! alas!   320
Where is thy head? where's that? Ay, me! where's
        that?
Pisanio might have kill'd thee at the heart,
And left this head on. How should this be? Pisanio?
'Tis he and Cloten; malice and lucre in them   324
Have laid this woe here. O! 'tis pregnant, pregnant!
The drug he gave me, which he said was precious
And cordial to me, have I not found it
Murderous to the senses? That confirms it home;   328
This is Pisanio's deed, and Cloten's: O!
Give colour to my pale cheek with thy blood,
That we the horrider may seem to those
Which chance to find us. O! my lord, my lord.   332
        [*Falls on the body.*]

*Enter Lucius, Captains, [other Officers,] and a
        Soothsayer.*

Cap. To them the legions garrison'd in Gallia,
After your will, have cross'd the sea, attending
You here at Milford-Haven with your ships:
They are in readiness.
        Luc.   But what from Rome?   336
        Cap. The senate hath stirr'd up the confiners

313 Hecuba; *cf. n.*   315 irregulous: *lawless*
325 pregnant: *obvious*   333 To them: *in addition to them*
337 confiners: *inhabitants*

And gentlemen of Italy, most willing spirits,
That promise noble service; and they come
Under the conduct of bold Iachimo,   340
Sienna's brother.

    Luc.   When expect you them?
    Cap. With the next benefit o' the wind.
    Luc.   This forwardness
Makes our hopes fair.   Command our present numbers
Be muster'd; bid the captains look to 't.   Now, sir, 344
What have you dream'd of late of this war's purpose?

    Sooth. Last night the very gods show'd me a vision,—
I fast and pray'd for their intelligence,—thus:
I saw Jove's bird, the Roman eagle, wing'd   348
From the spongy south to this part of the west,
There vanish'd in the sunbeams; which portends,
Unless my sins abuse my divination,
Success to the Roman host.

    Luc.   Dream often so,   352
And never false.   Soft, ho! what trunk is here
Without his top?   The ruin speaks that sometime
It was a worthy building.   How! a page!
Or dead or sleeping on him?   But dead rather,   356
For nature doth abhor to make his bed
With the defunct, or sleep upon the dead.
Let's see the boy's face.

    Cap.   He's alive, my lord.
    Luc. He'll, then, instruct us of this body.   Young
    one,   360
Inform us of thy fortunes, for it seems
They crave to be demanded.   Who is this
Thou mak'st thy bloody pillow?   Or who was he
That, otherwise than noble nature did,   364
Hath alter'd that good picture?   What's thy interest

349 spongy: *wet*   351 abuse: *pervert*
362 demanded: *inquired*   364, 365 otherwise . . . picture; *cf. n.*

In this sad wrack?   How came it?   Who is it?
What art thou?

    Imo.   I am nothing; or if not,
Nothing to be were better.   This was my master,   **368**
A very valiant Briton and a good,
That here by mountaineers lies slain.   Alas!
There are no more such masters; I may wander
From east to occident, cry out for service,   **372**
Try many, all good, serve truly, never
Find such another master.

    Luc.   'Lack, good youth!
Thou mov'st no less with thy complaining than
Thy master in bleeding.   Say his name, good friend.

    Imo. Richard du Champ.—[*Aside.*] If I do lie and
      do   **377**
No harm by it, though the gods hear, I hope
They'll pardon it.—Say you, sir?

    Luc.   Thy name?

    Imo.   Fidele, sir.

    Luc. Thou dost approve thyself the very same;   **380**
Thy name well fits thy faith, thy faith thy name.
Wilt take thy chance with me?   I will not say
Thou shalt be so well master'd, but be sure
No less belov'd.   The Roman emperor's letters,   **384**
Sent by a consul to me, should not sooner
Than thine own worth prefer thee.   Go with me.

    Imo. I'll follow, sir.   But first, an 't please the gods,
I'll hide my master from the flies, as deep   **388**
As these poor pickaxes can dig; and when
With wild wood-leaves and weeds I ha' strew'd his
      grave,
And on it said a century of prayers,

---

375 complaining: *mourning*   380 approve: *prove*
387 an 't: *if it*   389 poor pickaxes: *i.e. her fingers*
391 century: *hundred*

Such as I can, twice o'er, I'll weep and sigh;　　392
And, leaving so his service, follow you,
So please you entertain me.
　　Luc.　　　　　　　　　Ay, good youth,
And rather father thee than master thee.
My friends,　　396
The boy hath taught us manly duties; let us
Find out the prettiest daisied plot we can,
And make him with our pikes and partisans
A grave; come, arm him.　Boy, he is preferr'd　　400
By thee to us, and he shall be interr'd
As soldiers can.　Be cheerful; wipe thine eyes:
Some falls are means the happier to arise.　　*Exeunt.*

Scene Three

[*Cymbeline's Palace*]

Enter Cymbeline, Lords, Pisanio [and Attendants].

　　Cym. Again; and bring me word how 'tis with her.
　　　　　　　　　　　[*Exit an Attendant.*]
A fever with the absence of her son,
A madness, of which her life's in danger.　Heavens!
How deeply you at once do touch me.　Imogen,　　4
The great part of my comfort, gone; my queen
Upon a desperate bed, and in a time
When fearful wars point at me; her son gone,
So needful for this present: it strikes me, past　　8
The hope of comfort.　But for thee, fellow,
Who needs must know of her departure and
Dost seem so ignorant, we'll enforce it from thee

394 entertain: *take into service*
399 partisans: *combined spear and battle axe*
400 arm him: *carry him (i.e. the body of Cloten) in your arms*
4 touch: *wound*　　　　　8 present: *emergency*

By a sharp torture.

   Pis.   Sir, my life is yours,   12
I humbly set it at your will; but, for my mistress,
I nothing know where she remains, why gone,
Nor when she purposes return. Beseech your highness,
Hold me your loyal servant.

   1. Lord.   Good my liege,   16
The day that she was missing he was here;
I dare be bound he's true and shall perform
All parts of his subjection loyally. For Cloten,
There wants no diligence in seeking him,   20
And will, no doubt, be found.

   Cym.   The time is troublesome.
[*To Pisanio.*] We'll slip you for a season; but our jealousy
Does yet depend.

   1. Lord.   So please your majesty,
The Roman legions, all from Gallia drawn,   24
Are landed on your coast, with a supply
Of Roman gentlemen, by the senate sent.

   Cym Now for the counsel of my son and queen!
I am amaz'd with matter.

   1. Lord.   Good my liege,   28
Your preparation can affront no less
Than what you hear of; come more, for more you're ready:
The want is but to put those powers in motion
That long to move.

   Cym.   I thank you. Let's withdraw; 32
And meet the time as it seeks us. We fear not

16 Hold: *consider*   19 subjection: *service as a subject*
20 ·wants: *lacks*   22 slip you: *let you go*   jealousy: *suspicion*
23 depend: *remain in suspense*
28 amaz'd: *confused*   matter: *affairs of importance*
29 *Cf. n.*

What can from Italy annoy us, but
We grieve at chances here. Away!

Exeunt [all but Pisanio].

Pis. I heard no letter from my master since   36
I wrote him Imogen was slain; 'tis strange;
Nor hear I from my mistress, who did promise
To yield me often tidings; neither know I
What is betid to Cloten; but remain   40
Perplex'd in all: the heavens still must work.
Wherein I am false I am honest; not true to be true:
These present wars shall find I love my country,
Even to the note o' the king, or I'll fall in them.   44
All other doubts, by time let them be clear'd;
Fortune brings in some boats that are not steer'd.

Exit.

Scene Four

[Wales.   Before the Cave of Belarius]

Enter Belarius, Guiderius, and Arviragus.

Gui. The noise is round about us.
Bel.   Let us from it.
Arv. What pleasure, sir, find we in life, to lock it
From action and adventure?
Gui.   Nay, what hope
Have we in hiding us? this way, the Romans   4
Must or for Britons slay us, or receive us
For barbarous and unnatural revolts
During their use, and slay us after.
Bel.   Sons,
We'll higher to the mountains; there secure us.   8
To the king's party there's no going; newness

40 betid: *befallen*   43 find: *reveal*   44 note: *notice*
6 revolts: *rebels*   7 During their use: *while they can use us*

Of Cloten's death,—we being not known, not muster'd
Among the bands,—may drive us to a render
Where we have liv'd, and so extort from 's that   12
Which we have done, whose answer would be death
Drawn on with torture.

> *Gui.*   This is, sir, a doubt
In such a time nothing becoming you,
Nor satisfying us.

> *Arv.*   It is not likely   16
That when they hear the Roman horses neigh,
Behold their quarter'd fires, have both their eyes
And ears so cloy'd importantly as now,
That they will waste their time upon our note,   20
To know from whence we are.

> *Bel.*   O! I am known
Of many in the army; many years,
Though Cloten then but young, you see, not wore him
From my remembrance.   And, besides, the king   24
Hath not deserv'd my service nor your loves
Who find in my exile the want of breeding,
The certainty of this hard life; aye hopeless
To have the courtesy your cradle promis'd,   28
But to be still hot summer's tanlings and
The shrinking slaves of winter.

> *Gui.*   Than be so
Better to cease to be.   Pray, sir, to the army:
I and my brother are not known; yourself,   32
So out of thought, and thereto so o'ergrown,
Cannot be question'd.

> *Arv.*   By this sun that shines,

11 render: *account*   18 quarter'd fires: *camp fires*
19 cloy'd importantly: *crammed with matters of importance*
20 upon our note: *in noticing us*   27 aye: *forever*
29 tanlings: *creatures tanned by the sun*
33 thereto so o'ergrown: *also so overgrown with hair*

I'll thither: what thing is it that I never
Did see man die! scarce ever look'd on blood   36
But that of coward hares, hot goats, and venison!
Never bestrid a horse, save one that had
A rider like myself, who ne'er wore rowel
Nor iron on his heel! I am asham'd   40
To look upon the holy sun, to have
The benefit of his bless'd beams, remaining
So long a poor unknown.

   Gui.   By heavens! I'll go:
If you will bless me, sir, and give me leave,   44
I'll take the better care; but if you will not,
The hazard therefore due fall on me by
The hands of Romans.

   Arv.   So say I; amen.

   Bel. No reason I, since of your lives you set   48
So slight a valuation, should reserve
My crack'd one to more care. Have with you, boys!
If in your country wars you chance to die,
That is my bed too, lads, and there I'll lie: 52
Lead, lead.—[*Aside.*] The time seems long; their
    blood thinks scorn,
Till it fly out and show them princes born.   *Exeunt.*

35 what thing is it: *what a thing it is*
45 take . . . care: *have . . . protection*
53 thinks scorn: *despises everything*

ACT FIFTH

Scene One

[Britain.   The Roman Camp]

Enter Posthumus [with a bloody handkerchief].

Post. Yea, bloody cloth, I'll keep thee, for I wish'd
Thou shouldst be colour'd thus.   You married ones,
If each of you should take this course, how many
Must murder wives much better than themselves   4
For wrying but a little!   O Pisanio!
Every good servant does not all commands;
No bond but to do just ones.   Gods! if you
Should have ta'en vengeance on my faults, I never   8
Had liv'd to put on this; so had you sav'd
The noble Imogen to repent, and struck
Me, wretch more worth your vengeance.   But, alack!
You snatch some hence for little faults; that's love,   12
To have them fall no more; you some permit
To second ills with ills, each elder worse,
And make them dread it, to the doers' thrift.
But Imogen is your own; do your best wills,   16
And make me bless'd to obey.   I am brought hither
Among the Italian gentry, and to fight
Against my lady's kingdom; 'tis enough
That, Britain, I have kill'd thy mistress; peace!   20
I'll give no wound to thee.   Therefore good heavens,
Hear patiently my purpose: I'll disrobe me
Of these Italian weeds, and suit myself
As does a Briton peasant; so I'll fight   24
Against the part I come with, so I'll die

5 wrying: *swerving*   7 No bond: *there is no obligation*
9 put on: *instigate*   14 elder: *of later date*   15 *Cf. n.*
23 weeds: *garments*   suit: *dress*   25 part: *party*

For thee, O Imogen! even for whom my life
Is, every breath, a death: and thus, unknown,
Pitied nor hated, to the face of peril   28
Myself I'll dedicate.   Let me make men know
More valour in me than my habits show.
Gods! put the strength o' the Leonati in me.
To shame the guise o' the world, I will begin   32
The fashion, less without and more within.   *Exit.*

Scene Two

[*Field of Battle between the British and Roman
Camps*]

*Enter Lucius, Iachimo, and the Roman Army at one
door and the Britain army at another; Leonatus Posthumus following like a poor soldier. They march
over and go out. Then enter again in skirmish,
Iachimo and Posthumus; he vanquisheth and dis-
armeth Iachimo, and then leaves him.*

Iach. The heaviness and guilt within my bosom
Takes off my manhood: I have belied a lady,
The princess of this country, and the air on 't
Revengingly enfeebles me; or could this carl,   4
A very drudge of nature's, have subdu'd me
In my profession?   Knighthoods and honours, borne
As I wear mine, are titles but of scorn.
If that thy gentry, Britain, go before   8
This lout as he exceeds our lords, the odds
Is that we scarce are men and you are gods.

     Exit.

---

30 habits: *clothes*   32 guise: *custom*
1 heaviness and guilt: *i.e. the weight of guilt*   4 carl: *peasant*

The battle continues; the Britons fly; Cymbeline is taken. Then enter, to his rescue, Belarius, Guiderius, and Arvirugus.

 Bel. Stand, stand! We have the advantage of the ground.
The lane is guarded; nothing routs us but   12
The villainy of our fears.
 Gui. ⎱
 Arv. ⎰   Stand, stand, and fight!

Enter Posthumus, and seconds the Britons. They rescue Cymbeline, and exeunt. Then enter Lucius, Iachimo, and Imogen.

 Luc. Away, boy, from the troops, and save thyself;
For friends kill friends, and the disorder's such
As war were hoodwink'd.
 Iach.   'Tis their fresh supplies. 16
 Luc. It is a day turn'd strangely: or betimes
Let's reinforce, or fly.   *Exeunt.*

Scene Three

[Another Part of the Field]

Enter Posthumus and a Britain Lord.

 Lord. Cam'st thou from where they made the stand?
 Post.   I did:
Though you, it seems, come from the fliers.
 Lord.   I did.
 Post. No blame be to you, sir; for all was lost,
But that the heavens fought. The king himself   4
Of his wings destitute, the army broken,
And but the backs of Britons seen, all flying

16 hoodwink'd: *blindfolded*   17 betimes: *quickly*

Through a strait lane; the enemy full-hearted,
Lolling the tongue with slaughtering, having work　8
More plentiful than tools to do 't, struck down
Some mortally, some slightly touch'd, some falling
Merely through fear; that the strait pass was damm'd
With dead men hurt behind, and cowards living　12
To die with lengthen'd shame.

 Lord.   Where was this lane?

 Post. Close by the battle, ditch'd, and wall'd with
  turf;
Which gave advantage to an ancient soldier,
An honest one, I warrant; who deserv'd　16
So long a breeding as his white beard came to,
In doing this for his country; athwart the lane,
He, with two striplings,—lads more like to run
The country base than to commit such slaughter,—　20
With faces fit for masks, or rather fairer
Than those for preservation cas'd, or shame,
Made good the passage; cried to those that fled,
Our Britain's harts die flying, not our men:　24
To darkness fleet souls that fly backwards. Stand!
Or we are Romans, and will give you that
Like beasts which you shun beastly, and may save,
But to look back in frown: stand, stand!' These
  three,　28
Three thousand confident, in act as many,—
For three performers are the file when all
The rest do nothing,—with this word, 'Stand, stand!'
Accommodated by the place, more charming　32
With their own nobleness,— —which could have turn'd
A distaff to a lance,—gilded pale looks,

7 strait: *narrow*　20 country base: *country game of prisoners' base*
21 fit for: *i.e. beautiful enough to be protected by*
22 shame: *modesty*　　　　　　　　　　25 fleet: *vanish*
25-28 Stand . . . frown; *cf n.*　　29 confident: *in confidence*
30 file: *body of troops*　　　32 more charming: *charming others*

Part shame, part spirit renew'd; that some, turn'd
    coward
But by example,—O! a sin of war,   3
Damn'd in the first beginners,—'gan to look
The way that they did, and to grin like lions
Upon the pikes o' the hunters.   Then began
A stop i' the chaser, a retire, anon   4
A rout, confusion thick; forthwith they fly
Chickens the way which they stoop'd eagles; slaves,
The strides they victors made.   And now our cowards—
Like fragments in hard voyages—became   4
The life o' the need; having found the back door open
Of the unguarded hearts, Heavens! how they wound
Some slain before; some dying; some their friends
O'er-borne i' the former wave; ten, chas'd by one,   4
Are now each one the slaughter-man of twenty;
Those that would die or ere resist are grown
The mortal bugs o' the field!
    Lord.   This was strange chance
A narrow lane, an old man, and two boys!   5
    Post. Nay, do not wonder at it; you are made
Rather to wonder at the things you hear
Than to work any.   Will you rime upon 't,
And vent it for a mockery?   Here is one: 5
'Two boys, an old man twice a boy, a lane,
Preserv'd the Britons, was the Romans' bane.'
    Lord. Nay, be not angry, sir.
    Post.   'Lack! to what end
Who dares not stand his foe, I'll be his friend;   6
For if he'll do, as he is made to do,
I know he'll quickly fly my friendship too.
You have put me into rime.

42 stoop'd: *plunged*   42, 43 slaves . . . made; *cf.*
45 life o' the need: *what sustained life in time of need*
50 or ere: *sooner than*   51 bugs: *terror*

Lord.   Farewell; you're angry.   *Exit.*

Post. Still going?—This is a lord!   O noble misery!

To be i' the field, and ask, 'what news?' of me!   65

To-day how many would have given their honours

To have sav'd their carcasses! took heel to do 't,

And yet died too!   I, in mine own woe charm'd,   68

Could not find death where I did hear him groan,

Nor feel him where he struck: being an ugly monster,

'Tis strange he hides him in fresh cups, soft beds,

Sweet words; or hath more ministers than we   72

That draw his knives i' the war.   Well, I will find him;

For being now a favourer to the Briton,

No more a Briton, I have resum'd again

The part I came in; fight I will no more,   76

But yield me to the veriest hind that shall

Once touch my shoulder.   Great the slaughter is

Here made by the Roman; great the answer be

Britons must take.   For me, my ransom's death;   80

On either side I come to spend my breath,

Which neither here I'll keep nor bear again,

But end it by some means for Imogen.

Enter two [British] Captains, and Soldiers.

1. Cap. Great Jupiter be praised!   Lucius is taken.

'Tis thought the old man and his sons were angels.   85

2. Cap. There was a fourth man, in a silly habit,

That gave th' affront with them.

1. Cap.   So 'tis reported;

But none of 'em can be found.   Stand! who is there? 88

Post. A Roman,

Who had not now been drooping here, if seconds

Had answer'd him.

---

64 noble misery: *miserable nobility*   72 more: *other*
74 now: *but now*   77 hind: *menial*
86 silly: *simple*   87 affront: *attack*
90 seconds: *followers*   91 answer'd: *supported*

2. Cap.   Lay hands on him; a dog!
A leg of Rome shall not return to tell   92
What crows have peck'd them here. He brags his
    service
As if he were of note: bring him to the king.

*Enter Cymbeline, Belarius, Guiderius, Arviragus,
    Pisanio, and Roman Captives. The Captains pre-
    sent Posthumus to Cymbeline, who delivers him over
    to a Gaoler [then exeunt omnes].*

Scene Four

[Britain. A Prison]

Enter Posthumus and [two] Gaoler[s].

1. Gaol. You shall not now be stol'n, you have locks
    upon you;
So graze as you find pasture.
2. Gaol.   Ay, or a stomach.
                          [Exeunt Gaolers.]
Post. Most welcome, bondage! for thou art a way,
I think, to liberty. Yet am I better   4
Than one that's sick o' the gout, since he had rather
Groan so in perpetuity than be cur'd
By the sure physician death, who is the key
To unbar these locks. My conscience, thou art fetter'd
More than my shanks and wrists: you good gods, give
    me   9
The penitent instrument to pick that bolt;
Then, free for ever! Is 't enough I am sorry?
So children temporal fathers do appease;   12
Gods are more full of mercy. Must I repent?

1 *Cf. n.*   2 stomach: *appetite*
10 penitent instrument: *instrument of penance*
                                          11-17 *Cf. n.*

I cannot do it better than in gyves,
Desir'd more than constrain'd; to satisfy,
If of my freedom 'tis the main part, take   16
No stricter render of me than my all.
I know you are more clement than vile men,
Who of their broken debtors take a third,
A sixth, a tenth, letting them thrive again   20
On their abatement: that's not my desire;
For Imogen's dear life take mine; and though
'Tis not so dear, yet 'tis a life; you coin'd it;
'Tween man and man they weigh not every stamp;   24
Though light, take pieces for the figure's sake:
You rather mine, being yours; and so great powers,
If you will take this audit, take this life,
And cancel these cold bonds.   O Imogen!   28
I'll speak to thee in silence.   [*Sleeps.*]

*Solemn music. Enter, as in an apparition, Sicilius
Leonatus, father to Posthumus, an old man, attired
like a warrior; leading in his hand an ancient matron,
his wife, and mother to Posthumus, with music before
them. Then, after other music, follow the two
young Leonati, brothers to Posthumus, with wounds,
as they died in the wars. They circle Posthumus
round, as he lies sleeping.*

Sici.   No more, thou thunder-master, show
          Thy spite on mortal flies:
       With Mars fall out, with Juno chide,   32
          That thy adulteries
             Rates and revenges.
       Hath my poor boy done aught but well,
          Whose face I never saw?   36

14 gyves: *fetters*   21 abatement: *diminished capital*
24 stamp: *coin*   26 You rather . . . yours; *cf. n.*
30 thunder-master: *Jupiter*   34 Rates: *chides*

I died whilst in the womb he stay'd
　　Attending nature's law:
Whose father then—as men report,
　　Thou orphans' father art—　　　　　　　40
Thou shouldst have been, and shielded him
　　From this earth-vexing smart.

Moth. Lucina lent not me her aid,
　　But took me in my throes;　　　　　　　44
That from me was Posthumus ript,
　　Came crying 'mongst his foes,
　　　　A thing of pity!

Sici. Great nature, like his ancestry,　　48
　　Moulded the stuff so fair,
That he deserv'd the praise o' the world,
　　As great Sicilius' heir.

1. Bro. When once he was mature for man,　52
　　In Britain where was he
That could stand up his parallel,
　　Or fruitful object be
In eye of Imogen, that best　　　　　　　56
　　Could deem his dignity?

Moth. With marriage wherefore was he mock'd,
　　To be exil'd, and thrown
From Leonati seat, and cast　　　　　　60
　　From her his dearest one,
　　　　Sweet Imogen?

Sici. Why did you suffer Iachimo,
　　Slight thing of Italy,　　　　　　　　64
To taint his nobler heart and brain
　　With needless jealousy;
And to become the geck and scorn
　　O' the other's villainy?　　　　　　　68

---

38 Attending: *awaiting*
43 Lucina: *goddess who assists in childbirth*
57 deem: *judge*　　　　　　　　　　　67 geck: *fool*

2. Bro. For this from stiller seats we came,
   Our parents and us twain,
   That striking in our country's cause
   Fell bravely and were slain;   72
   Our fealty and Tenantius' right
   With honour to maintain.

1. Bro. Like hardiment Posthumus hath
   To Cymbeline perform'd: 76
   Then Jupiter, thou king of gods,
   Why hast thou thus adjourn'd
   The graces for his merits due,
   Being all to dolours turn'd?   80

Sici. Thy crystal window ope; look out;
   No longer exercise
   Upon a valiant race thy harsh
   And potent injuries.   84

Moth. Since, Jupiter, our son is good,
   Take off his miseries.

Sici. Peep through thy marble mansion; help!
   Or we poor ghosts will cry   88
   To the shining synod of the rest
   Against thy deity.

Both Bro. Help, Jupiter! or we appeal,
   And from thy justice fly.   92

*Jupiter descends in thunder and lightning, sitting upon
an eagle: he throws a thunderbolt. The Ghosts fall
on their knees.*

Jup. No more, you petty spirits of region low,
   Offend our hearing; hush! How dare you ghosts
Accuse the thunderer, whose bolt, you know,
   Sky-planted, batters all rebelling coasts?   96
Poor shadows of Elysium, hence; and rest

---

75 hardiment: *deeds of valor*   78 adjourn'd: *delayed*
80 dolours: *sorrows*   89 synod: *assembly of gods*

Upon your never-withering banks of flowers:
Be not with mortal accidents opprest;
  No care of yours it is; you know 'tis ours.   100
Whom best I love I cross, to make my gift,
  The more delay'd, delighted. Be content;
Your low-laid son our godhead will uplift:
  His comforts thrive, his trials well are spent.   104
Our Jovial star reign'd at his birth, and in
  Our temple was he married. Rise, and fade!
He shall be lord of Lady Imogen,
  And happier much by his affliction made.   108
This tablet lay upon his breast, wherein
  Our pleasure his full fortune doth confine;
And so, away: no further with your din
  Express impatience, lest you stir up mine.   112
  Mount, eagle, to my palace crystalline.   *Ascends.*
  Sici. He came in thunder; his celestial breath
Was sulphurous to smell; the holy eagle
Stoop'd, as to foot us; his ascension is   116
More sweet than our bless'd fields; his royal bird
Prunes the immortal wing and cloys his beak,
As when his god is pleas'd.
  All.   Thanks, Jupiter!
  Sici. The marble pavement closes; he is enter'd 120
His radiant roof. Away! and, to be blest,
Let us with care perform his great behest.
                    [The Ghosts] vanish.
  Post. [*Awaking.*] Sleep, thou hast been a grandsire,
    and begot
A father to me; and thou hast created   124
A mother and two brothers. But—O scorn!—
Gone! they went hence so soon as they were born:

102 delighted: *delightful*
116 as to foot us: *as if to seize us in his talons*
118 Prunes: *preens*   cloys: *claws*   120 marble pavement: *sky*

And so I am awake. Poor wretches, that depend
On greatness' favour dream as I have done;   128
Wake, and find nothing. But, alas! I swerve:
Many dream not to find, neither deserve,
And yet are steep'd in favours; so am I,
That have this golden chance and know not why.   132
What fairies haunt this ground? A book? O rare
    one!
Be not, as is our fangled world, a garment
Nobler than that it covers: let thy effects
So follow, to be most unlike our courtiers,   136
As good as promise.   *Reads.*
    'Whenas a lion's whelp shall, to himself un-
    known, without seeking find, and be embraced
    by a piece of tender air; and when from a 140
    stately cedar shall be lopped branches, which,
    being dead many years, shall after revive, be
    jointed to the old stock, and freshly grow, then
    shall Posthumus end his miseries, Britain be 144
    fortunate, and flourish in peace and plenty.'
'Tis still a dream, or else such stuff as madmen
Tongue and brain not; either both or nothing;
Or senseless speaking, or a speaking such   148
As sense cannot untie. Be what it is,
The action of my life is like it, which
I'll keep, if but for sympathy.

Enter Gaoler.

    Gaol. Come, sir, are you ready for 152
death?
    Post. Over-roasted rather; ready long ago.

129 swerve: *err*   133 book: *writing*
134 fangled: *fond of finery*   138 Whenas: *when*
147 Tongue: *speak*   brain: *understand*

Gaol. Hanging is the word, sir: if you be ready for that, you are well cooked.   156

Post. So, if I prove a good repast to the spectators, the dish pays the shot.

Gaol. A heavy reckoning for you, sir; but the comfort is, you shall be called to no 160 more payments, fear no more tavern-bills, which are often the sadness of parting, as the procuring of mirth. You come in faint for want of meat, depart reeling with too much drink, sorry 164 that you have paid too much; and sorry that you are paid too much; purse and brain both empty; the brain the heavier for being too light, the purse too light, being drawn of heaviness: 168 of this contradiction you shall now be quit. O! the charity of a penny cord; it sums up thousands in a trice: you have no true debitor and creditor but it; of what's past, is, and to come, 172 the discharge. Your neck, sir, is pen, book and counters; so the acquittance follows.

Post. I am merrier to die than thou art to live.

Gaol. Indeed, sir, he that sleeps feels 176 not the toothache; but a man that were to sleep your sleep, and a hangman to help him to bed, I think he would change places with his officer; for look you, sir, you know not which way you 180 shall go.

Post. Yes, indeed do I, fellow.

Gaol. Your death has eyes in 's head, then; I have not seen him so pictur'd: you 184 must either be directed by some that take upon them to know, or take upon yourself that which

---

156 well cooked; *cf. n*
183 death: *i.e. a death's head or skull*

158 the dish . . . shot; *cf. n.*
185 take upon: *pretend*

I am sure you do not know, or jump the after
inquiry on your own peril: and how you shall 188
speed in your journey's end, I think you'll never
return to tell one.

Post. I tell thee, fellow, there are none want
eyes to direct them the way I am going but such 192
as wink and will not use them.

Gaol. What an infinite mock is this,
that a man should have the best use of eyes to
see the way of blindness! I am sure hanging's 196
the way of winking.

Enter a Messenger.

Mess. Knock off his manacles; bring your
prisoner to the king.

Post. Thou bring'st good news; I am called 200
to be made free.

Gaol. I'll be hang'd, then.

Post. Thou shalt be then freer than a gaoler;
no bolts for the dead.   204
Exeunt [all but Gaoler].

Gaol. Unless a man would marry a
gallows and beget young gibbets, I never saw
one so prone. Yet, on my conscience, there are
verier knaves desire to live, for all he be a 208
Roman; and there be some of them too that
die against their wills; so should I, if I were
one. I would we were all of one mind, and
one mind good; O! there were desolation of 212
gaolers and gallowses. I speak against my present profit, but my wish hath a preferment in 't.

Exit.

187 jump: *risk*   189 speed: *fare*
193 wink: *shut their eyes*   207 prone: *eager*
214 hath a preferment; *cf. n.*

Scene Five

[*Cymbeline's Tent*]

*Enter Cymbeline, Belarius, Guiderius, Arviragus,
    Pisanio, Lords [Officers, and Attendants].*

Cym. Stand by my side, you whom the gods have
    made
Preservers of my throne.   Woe is my heart
That the poor soldier that so richly fought,
Whose rags sham'd gilded arms, whose naked breast   4
Stepp'd before targes of proof, cannot be found:
He shall be happy that can find him, if
Our grace can make him so.
    Bel.   I never saw
Such noble fury in so poor a thing;   8
Such precious deeds in one that promis'd nought
But beggary and poor looks.
    Cym.   No tidings of him?
    Pis. He hath been search'd among the dead and
    living,
But no trace of him.
    Cym.   To my grief, I am   12
The heir of his reward; which I will add
            [*To Belarius, Guiderius, and Arviragus.*]
To you, the liver, heart, and brain of Britain,
By whom, I grant, she lives. 'Tis now the time
To ask of whence you are; report it.
    Bel.   Sir,   16
In Cambria are we born, and gentlemen:
Further to boast were neither true nor modest,
Unless I add, we are honest.
    Cym.   Bow your knees.

5 targes: *shields*   11 search'd: *sought*
17 Cambria: *Wales*

Arise, my knights o' the battle: I create you   20
Companions to our person, and will fit you
With dignities becoming your estates.

Enter Cornelius and Ladies.

There's business in these faces.   Why so sadly
Greet you our victory? you look like Romans,   24
And not o' the court of Britain.

Cor.   Hail, great king!
To sour your happiness, I must report
The queen is dead.

Cym.   Whom worse than a physician
Would this report become?   But I consider,   28
By medicine life may be prolong'd, yet death
Will seize the doctor too.   How ended she?

Cor. With horror, madly dying, like her life;
Which, being cruel to the world, concluded   32
Most cruel to herself.   What she confess'd
I will report, so please you: these her women
Can trip me if I err, who with wet cheeks
Were present when she finish'd.

Cym.   Prithee, say.   36

Cor. First, she confess'd she never lov'd you, only
Affected greatness got by you, not you;
Married your royalty, was wife to your place;
Abhorr'd your person.

Cym.   She alone knew this;   40
And, but she spoke it dying, I would not
Believe her lips in opening it.   Proceed.

Cor. Your daughter, whom she bore in hand to love
With such integrity, she did confess   44
Was as a scorpion to her sight; whose life,

28 consider: *remember*   38 Affected: *desired*
42 opening: *revealing*   43 bore in hand: *pretended*

But that her flight prevented it, she had
Ta'en off by poison.

 Cym.   O most delicate fiend!
Who is 't can read a woman? Is there more? 48
 Cor. More, sir, and worse. She did confess she had
For you a mortal mineral; which, being took,
Should by the minute feed on life, and ling'ring,
By inches waste you; in which time she purpos'd, 52
By watching, weeping, tendance, kissing, to
O'ercome you with her show; yea, and in time—
When she had fitted you with her craft—to work
Her son into the adoption of the crown; 56
But failing of her end by his strange absence,
Grew shameless-desperate; open'd, in despite
Of heaven and men, her purposes; repented
The evils she hatch'd were not effected: so, 60
Despairing died.

 Cym.   Heard you all this, her women?
 1. Lady. We did, so please your highness.
 Cym.   Mine eyes
Were not in fault, for she was beautiful;
Mine ears, that heard her flattery; nor my heart, 64
That thought her like her seeming: it had been vicious
To have mistrusted her: yet, O my daughter!
That it was folly in me, thou mayst say,
And prove it in thy feeling. Heaven mend all! 68

*Enter Lucius, Iachimo, the Soothsayer, and other
Roman Prisoners: Posthumus behind, and Imogen.*

Thou com'st not, Caius, now for tribute; that
The Britons have raz'd out, though with the loss
Of many a bold one; whose kinsmen have made suit 71

46 prevented: *anticipated*   47 delicate: *artful*
50 mortal mineral: *deadly poison*   55 fitted: *prepared*
65 vicious: *wrong*   70 raz'd: *blotted*

That their good souls may be appeas'd with slaughter
Of you their captives, which ourself have granted:
So, think of your estate.

   Luc. Consider, sir, the chance of war: the day
Was yours by accident; had it gone with us,   76
We should not, when the blood was cool, have
     threaten'd
Our prisoners with the sword. But since the gods
Will have it thus, that nothing but our lives
May be call'd ransom, let it come; sufficeth,   80
A Roman with a Roman's heart can suffer;
Augustus lives to think on 't; and so much
For my peculiar care. This one thing only
I will entreat; my boy, a Briton born,   84
Let him be ransom'd; never master had
A page so kind, so duteous, diligent,
So tender over his occasions, true,
So feat, so nurse-like. Let his virtue join   88
With my request, which I'll make bold your highness
Cannot deny; he hath done no Briton harm,
Though he have serv'd a Roman. Save him, sir,
And spare no blood beside.   92

   Cym. I have surely seen him;
His favour is familiar to me. Boy,
Thou hast look'd thyself into my grace,
And art mine own. I know not why nor wherefore 96
To say, 'live, boy': ne'er thank thy master; live:
And ask of Cymbeline what boon thou wilt,
Fitting my bounty and thy state, I'll give it;
Yea, though thou do demand a prisoner,   100
The noblest ta'en.

74 estate: *situation*   80 sufficeth: *it suffices*
83 peculiar: *personal*
87 So tender . . . occasions: *so considerate in attending to his duties*
88 feat: *dextrous*   virtue: *merit*

Imo.   I humbly thank your highness.
Luc. I do not bid thee beg my life, good lad;
And yet I know thou wilt.
Imo.   No, no; alack!
There's other work in hand. I see a thing   104
Bitter to me as death; your life, good master,
Must shuffle for itself.
Luc.   The boy disdains me,
He leaves me, scorns me; briefly die their joys
That place them on the truth of girls and boys.   108
Why stands he so perplex'd?
Cym.   What wouldst thou, boy?
I love thee more and more; think more and more
What's best to ask. Know'st him thou look'st on?
        speak;
Wilt have him live? Is he thy kin? thy friend?   112
Imo. He is a Roman; no more kin to me
Than I to your highness; who, being born your vassal,
Am something nearer.
Cym.   Wherefore ey'st him so?
Imo. I'll tell you, sir, in private, if you please   116
To give me hearing.
Cym.   Ay, with all my heart,
And lend my best attention. What's thy name?
Imo. Fidele, sir.
Cym.   Thou'rt my good youth, my page;
I'll be thy master: walk with me; speak freely.   120
        [*Cymbeline and Imogen converse apart.*]
Bel. Is not this boy reviv'd from death?
Arv.   One sand another
Not more resembles;—that sweet rosy lad
Who died, and was Fidele. What think you?
Gui. The same dead thing alive.   124

104 a thing: *i.e. the ring on Iachimo's finger*

Bel. Peace, peace! see further; he eyes us not; for-
    bear;
Creatures may be alike; were 't he, I am sure
He would have spoke to us.
    Gui.   But we saw him dead.
    Bel. Be silent; let's see further.
    Pis.   [*Aside.*] It is my mistress: 128
Since she is living, let the time run on
To good, or bad.
           [*Cymbeline and Imogen come forward.*]
    Cym. [*To Imogen.*] Come, stand thou by our side:
Make thy demand aloud.—[*To Iachimo.*] Sir, step you
    forth;
Give answer to this boy, and do it freely,   132
Or, by our greatness and the grace of it,
Which is our honour, bitter torture shall
Winnow the truth from falsehood.—[*To Imogen.*] On,
    speak to him.
    Imo. My boon is, that this gentleman may render 136
Of whom he had this ring.
    Post.   [*Aside.*] What's that to him?
    Cym. That diamond upon your finger, say
How came it yours?
    Iach. Thou'lt torture me to leave unspoken that 140
Which, to be spoke, would torture thee.
    Cym.   How! me?
    Iach. I am glad to be constrain'd to utter that
Which torments me to conceal.   By villainy
I got this ring; 'twas Leonatus' jewel,   144
Whom thou didst banish, and—which more may grieve
    thee,
As it doth me—a nobler sir ne'er liv'd

140 to leave: *for leaving*

'Twixt sky and ground. Wilt thou hear more, my
    lord?
  Cym. All that belongs to this.
  Iach.   That paragon, thy daughter,— 148
For whom my heart drops blood, and my false spirits
Quail to remember,—Give me leave; I faint.
  Cym. My daughter! what of her? Renew thy
    strength;
I had rather thou shouldst live while nature will   152
Than die ere I hear more. Strive, man, and speak.
  Iach. Upon a time,—unhappy was the clock
That struck the hour!—it was in Rome,—accurs'd
The mansion where!—'twas at a feast—O, would   156
Our viands had been poison'd, or at least
Those which I heav'd to head!—the good Post-
    humus,—
What should I say? he was too good to be
Where ill men were; and was the best of all   160
Amongst the rar'st of good ones;—sitting sadly
Hearing us praise our loves of Italy
For beauty that made barren the swell'd boast
Of him that best could speak; for feature laming   164
The shrine of Venus, or straight-pight Minerva,
Postures beyond brief nature; for condition,
A shop of all the qualities that man
Loves woman for; besides that hook of wiving,   168
Fairness which strikes the eye.
  Cym.   I stand on fire.
Come to the matter.
  Iach.   All too soon I shall,

---

161 sadly: *soberly*
164 feature: *proportion of parts*   laming: *making seem deformed*
165 shrine: *statue*   straight-pight: *erect*
166 Postures . . . nature; *cf. n.*   condition: *character*
167 shop: *storehouse*
                       168 hook of wiving; *cf. n.*

Unless thou wouldst grieve quickly.   This Post-
    humus—
Most like a noble lord in love, and one   172
That had a royal lover—took his hint;
And, not dispraising whom we prais'd,—therein
He was as calm as virtue,—he began
His mistress' picture; which by his tongue being
    made,   176
And then a mind put in 't, either our brags
Were crack'd of kitchen trulls, or his description
Prov'd us unspeaking sots.
   Cym.   Nay, nay, to the purpose.
   Iach. Your daughter's chastity, there it begins.   180
He spake of her as Dian had hot dreams,
And she alone were cold; whereat I, wretch,
Made scruple of his praise, and wager'd with him
Pieces of gold 'gainst this, which then he wore   184
Upon his honour'd finger, to attain
In suit the place of his bed, and win this ring
By hers and mine adultery.   He, true knight,
No lesser of her honour confident   188
Than I did truly find her, stakes this ring;
And would so, had it been a carbuncle
Of Phœbus' wheel; and might so safely, had it
Been all the worth of 's car.   Away to Britain   192
Post I in this design.   Well may you, sir,
Remember me at court, where I was taught
Of your chaste daughter the wide difference
'Twixt amorous and villainous.   Being thus quench'd
Of hope, not longing, mine Italian brain   197

178 crack'd: *uttered boastfully*   trulls: *sluts*
179 unspeaking sots: *fools incapable of speech*
181 as: *as if, in comparison*
183 Made scruple: *expressed doubt*   186 In suit: *by suing*
191 Of Phœbus' wheel: *from the wheel of the chariot of the sun*
192 car: *chariot*

'Gan in your duller Britain operate
Most vilely; for my vantage, excellent;
And, to be brief, my practice so prevail'd,   200
That I return'd with simular proof enough
To make the noble Leonatus mad,
By wounding his belief in her renown
With tokens thus, and thus; averring notes   204
Of chamber-hanging, pictures, this her bracelet;—
Oh cunning! how I got it!—nay, some marks
Of secret on her person, that he could not
But think her bond of chastity quite crack'd,   208
I having ta'en the forfeit. Whereupon,—
Methinks I see him now,—
          Post. [Coming forward.] Ay, so thou dost,
Italian fiend!—Ay me, most credulous fool,
Egregious murderer, thief, anything   212
That's due to all the villains past, in being,
To come. O! give me cord, or knife, or poison,
Some upright justicer. Thou king, send out
For torturers ingenious; it is I   216
That all the abhorred things o' the earth amend
By being worse than they. I am Posthumus,
That kill'd thy daughter; villain-like, I lie;
That caus'd a lesser villain than myself,   220
A sacrilegious thief, to do 't; the temple
Of virtue was she; yea, and she herself.
Spit, and throw stones, cast mire upon me, set
The dogs o' the street to bay me; every villain   224
Be call'd Posthumus Leonatus; and
Be villainy less than 'twas! O Imogen!
My queen, my life, my wife! O Imogen,
Imogen, Imogen!

200 practice: *stratagem*   201 simular: *specious*
203 renown: *good name*   204 averring: *avouching*
217 amend: *make seem less vile*   222 she herself: *i.e. virtue herself*

Imo.   Peace, my lord! hear, hear!   228
Post. Shall's have a play of this?   Thou scornful page,
There lie thy part.   [*Striking her: she falls.*]
Pis.   O, gentlemen, help!
Mine, and your mistress!   O! my Lord Posthumus,
You ne'er kill'd Imogen till now.   Help, help!   232
Mine honour'd lady!
Cym.   Does the world go round?
Post. How come these staggers on me?
Pis.   Wake, my mistress!
Cym. If this be so, the gods do mean to strike me
To death with mortal joy.
Pis.   How fares my mistress? 236
Imo. O! get thee from my sight:
Thou gav'st me poison: dangerous fellow, hence!
Breathe not where princes are.
Cym.   The tune of Imogen!
Pis. Lady,   240
The gods throw stones of sulphur on me, if
That box I gave you was not thought by me
A precious thing: I had it from the queen.
Cym. New matter still?
Imo.   It poison'd me.
Cor.   O gods! 244
I left out one thing which the queen confess'd,
Which must approve thee honest: 'If Pisanio
Have,' said she, 'given his mistress that confection
Which I gave him for cordial, she is serv'd   248
As I would serve a rat.'
Cym.   What's this, Cornelius?
Cor. The queen, sir, very oft importun'd me

234 staggers: *dizziness*   239 tune: *voice*
241 stones of sulphur: *thunderbolts*

To temper poisons for her, still pretending
The satisfaction of her knowledge only 252
In killing creatures vile, as cats and dogs,
Of no esteem; I, dreading that her purpose
Was of more danger, did compound for her
A certain stuff, which, being ta'en, would cease 256
The present power of life, but in short time
All offices of nature should again
Do their due functions. Have you ta'en of it?

   Imo. Most like I did, for I was dead.

   Bel.   My boys, 260
There was our error.

   Gui.   This is, sure, Fidele.

   Imo. Why did you throw your wedded lady from
     you?
Think that you are upon a rock; and now
Throw me again.   *[Embracing him.]*

   Post.   Hang there like fruit, my soul, 264
Till the tree die!

   Cym.   How now, my flesh, my child!
What, mak'st thou me a dullard in this act?
Wilt thou not speak to me?

   Imo. [Kneeling.]   Your blessing, sir.

   Bel. [To Guiderius and Arviragus.] Though you did
     love this youth, I blame ye not; 268
You had a motive for 't.

   Cym.   My tears that fall
Prove holy water on thee! Imogen,
Thy mother's dead.

   Imo.   I am sorry for 't, my lord.

   Cym. O, she was naught; and long of her it was 272
That we meet here so strangely; but her son

251 temper: *compound*   263 rock: *precipice*
268 blame ye not: *i.e. am not surprised*   269 motive: *reason*
272 naught: *worthless*   long of: *because of*

Is gone, we know not how, nor where.

  Pis.   My lord,

Now fear is from me, I'll speak troth.   Lord Cloten,

Upon my lady's missing, came to me   276

With his sword drawn, foam'd at the mouth, and swore

If I discover'd not which way she was gone,

It was my instant death.   By accident,

I had a feigned letter of my master's   280

Then in my pocket, which directed him

To seek her on the mountains near to Milford;

Where, in a frenzy, in my master's garments,

Which he enforc'd from me, away he posts   284

With unchaste purpose and with oath to violate

My lady's honour; what became of him

I further know not.

  Gui.   Let me end the story:

I slew him there.

  Cym.   Marry, the gods forfend!   288

I would not thy good deeds should from my lips

Pluck a hard sentence: prithee, valiant youth,

Deny 't again.

  Gui.   I have spoke it, and I did it.

  Cym. He was a prince.   292

  Gui. A most incivil one.   The wrongs he did me

Were nothing princelike; for he did provoke me

With language that would make me spurn the sea

If it could so roar to me.   I cut off 's head;   296

And am right glad he is not standing here

To tell this tale of mine.

  Cym.   I am sorry for thee:

By thine own tongue thou art condemn'd, and must

Endure our law.   Thou'rt dead.

  Imo.   That headless man 300

275 troth: *truth*   288 forfend: *forbid*

I thought had been my lord.

Cym.   Bind the offender,
And take him from our presence.

Bel.   Stay, sir king:
This man is better than the man he slew,
As well descended as thyself; and hath   304
More of thee merited than a band of Clotens
Had ever scar for. [*To the Guard.*] Let his arms alone;
They were not born for bondage.

Cym.   Why, old soldier,
Wilt thou undo the worth thou art unpaid for   308
By tasting of our wrath? How of descent
As good as we?

Arv.   In that he spake too far.

Cym. And thou shalt die for 't.

Bel.   We will die all three:
But I will prove that two on 's are as good   312
As I have given out him. My sons, I must
For mine own part unfold a dangerous speech,
Though, haply, well for you.

Arv.   Your danger's ours.

Gui. And our good his.

Bel.   Have at it, then, by leave. 316
Thou hadst, great king, a subject who was call'd
Belarius.

Cym.   What of him? he is
A banish'd traitor.

Bel.   He it is that hath
Assum'd this age: indeed, a banish'd man;   320
I know not how a traitor.

Cym.   Take him hence:
The whole world shall not save him.

Bel.   Not too hot:

304-306 hath . . . scar for; *cf. n.*   320 Assum'd: *attained*

First pay me for the nursing of thy sons;
And let it be confiscate all so soon   324
As I have receiv'd it.
 Cym.   Nursing of my sons!
 Bel. I am too blunt and saucy; here's my knee:
Ere I arise I will prefer my sons;
Then spare not the old father. Mighty sir,   328
These two young gentlemen, that call me father,
And think they are my sons, are none of mine;
They are the issue of your loins, my liege,
And blood of your begetting.
 Cym.   How! my issue!   332
 Bel. So sure as you your father's. I, old Morgan,
Am that Belarius whom you sometime banish'd:
Your pleasure was my mere offence, my punishment
Itself, and all my treason; that I suffer'd   336
Was all the harm I did. These gentle princes—
For such and so they are—these twenty years
Have I train'd up; those arts they have as I
Could put into them; my breeding was, sir, as   340
Your highness knows. Their nurse, Euriphile,
Whom for the theft I wedded, stole these children
Upon my banishment: I mov'd her to 't,
Having receiv'd the punishment before,   344
For that which I did then; beaten for loyalty
Excited me to treason. Their dear loss,
The more of you 'twas felt the more it shap'd
Unto my end of stealing them. But, gracious sir,   348
Here are your sons again; and I must lose
Two of the sweet'st companions in the world.
The benediction of these covering heavens
Fall on their heads like dew! for they are worthy   352

335 pleasure: *caprice* mere: *sole*
345 beaten: *i.e. my being beaten*   346 dear: *great*
347, 348 shap'd . . . end: *fitted my purpose*

To inlay heaven with stars.

Cym.   Thou weep'st, and speak'st.
The service that you three have done is more
Unlike than this thou tell'st.   I lost my children:
If these be they, I know not how to wish   356
A pair of worthier sons.

Bel.   Be pleas'd awhile.
This gentleman, whom I call Polydore,
Most worthy prince, as yours, is true Guiderius;
This gentleman, my Cadwal, Arviragus,   360
Your younger princely son; he, sir, was lapp'd
In a most curious mantle, wrought by the hand
Of his queen mother, which, for more probation,
I can with ease produce.

Cym.   Guiderius had   364
Upon his neck a mole, a sanguine star;
It was a mark of wonder.

Bel.   This is he,
Who hath upon him still that natural stamp.
It was wise nature's end in the donation,   368
To be his evidence now.

Cym.   O! what, am I
A mother to the birth of three?   Ne'er mother
Rejoic'd deliverance more.   Blest pray you be,
That, after this strange starting from your orbs,   372
You may reign in them now.   O Imogen!
Thou hast lost by this a kingdom.

Imo.   No, my lord;
I have got two worlds by 't.   O my gentle brothers!
Have we thus met?   O, never say hereafter   376
But I am truest speaker: you call'd me brother,
When I was but your sister; I you brothers

354, 355 The service . . . tell'st; *cf. n.*   361 lapp'd: *wrapped*
363 probation: *proof*   371 Rejoic'd: *joyed in*

When ye were so indeed.

    Cym.   Did you e'er meet?

    Arv. Ay, my good lord.

    Gui.   And at first meeting lov'd; 380

Continued so, until we thought he died.

    Cor. By the queen's dram she swallow'd.

    Cym.   O rare instinct!

When shall I hear all through?   This fierce abridg-
      ment

Hath to it circumstantial branches, which   384

Distinction should be rich in.   Where? how liv'd you?

And when came you to serve our Roman captive?

How parted with your brothers? how first met them?

Why fled you from the court, and whither?   These, 388

And your three motives to the battle, with

I know not how much more, should be demanded,

And all the other by-dependances,

From chance to chance, but nor the time nor place 392

Will serve our long interrogatories.   See,

Posthumus anchors upon Imogen,

And she, like harmless lightning, throws her eye

On him, her brothers, me, her master, hitting   396

Each object with a joy: the counterchange

Is severally in all.   Let's quit this ground,

And smoke the temple with our sacrifices.

[*To Belarius.*] Thou art my brother; so we'll hold thee
      ever.   400

    Imo. You are my father too; and did relieve me,

To see this gracious season.

    Cym.   All o'erjoy'd

Save these in bonds; let them be joyful too,

For they shall taste our comfort.

383 fierce abridgment: *rapid narration*
385 Distinction . . . rich in; *cf. n.*
391 by-dependances: *side-issues*
397, 398 the counterchange . . . all; *cf. n.*

389 your three: *of you three*
396 her master: *i.e. Lucius*

Imo.   My good master, 404
I will yet do you service.
  Luc.   Happy be you!
  Cym. The forlorn soldier, that so nobly fought,
He would have well becom'd this place and grac'd
The thankings of a king.
  Post.   I am, sir,   408
The soldier that did company these three
In poor beseeming; 'twas a fitment for
The purpose I then follow'd. That I was he,
Speak, Iachimo; I had you down and might   412
Have made you finish.
  Iach.   [*Kneeling.*] I am down again;
But now my heavy conscience sinks my knee,
As then your force did. Take that life, beseech you,
Which I so often owe, but your ring first,   416
And here the bracelet of the truest princess
That ever swore her faith.
  Post.   Kneel not to me:
The power that I have on you is to spare you;
The malice towards you to forgive you. Live,   420
And deal with others better.
  Cym.   Nobly doom'd:
We'll learn our freeness of a son-in-law;
Pardon's the word to all.
  Arv.   You holp us, sir,
As you did mean indeed to be our brother;   424
Joy'd are we that you are.
  Post. Your servant, princes. Good my lord of Rome,
Call forth your soothsayer. As I slept, methought
Great Jupiter, upon his eagle back'd,   428
Appear'd to me, with other spritely shows

---

410 beseeming: *appearance*   fitment: *preparation*
413 finish: *die*   421 doom'd: *judged*
422 freeness: *generosity*   429 spritely shows: *ghostly apparitions*

Of mine own kindred: when I wak'd, I found
This label on my bosom; whose containing
Is so from sense in hardness that I can   432
Make no collection of it; let him show
His skill in the construction.

 Luc.   Philarmonus!
 Sooth. Here, my good lord.
 Luc.   Read, and declare the meaning.
 Sooth. [*Reads.*] 'Whenas a lion's whelp shall, 436
to himself unknown, without seeking find, and be
embraced by a piece of tender air; and when from
a stately cedar shall be lopped branches, which,
being dead many years, shall after revive, be 440
jointed to the old stock, and freshly grow: then
shall Posthumus end his miseries, Britain be
fortunate, and flourish in peace and plenty.'

Thou, Leonatus, art the lion's whelp;   444
The fit and apt construction of thy name,
Being Leo-natus, doth import so much.
[*To Cymbeline.*] The piece of tender air, thy virtuous
 daughter,
Which we call *mollis aer;* and *mollis aer*   448
We term it *mulier;* which *mulier,* I divine,
Is this most constant wife; who, even now,
Answering the letter of the oracle,
Unknown to you, [*To Posthumus.*] unsought, were
 clipp'd about   452
With this most tender air.

 Cym.   This hath some seeming.
 Sooth. The lofty cedar, royal Cymbeline,
Personates thee, and thy lopp'd branches point
Thy two sons forth; who, by Belarius stolen,   456

431 containing: *contents*   432 from sense: *incomprehensible*
433 collection: *deduction*   448 mollis aer: *tender air*
452 clipp'd: *clasped*

For many years thought dead, are now reviv'd,
To the majestic cedar join'd, whose issue
Promises Britain peace and plenty.
   Cym.   Well;
My peace we will begin. And, Caius Lucius,   460
Although the victor, we submit to Cæsar,
And to the Roman empire; promising
To pay our wonted tribute, from the which
We were dissuaded by our wicked queen;   464
Whom heavens—in justice both on her and hers—
Have laid most heavy hand.
   Sooth. The fingers of the powers above do tune
The harmony of this peace. The vision,   468
Which I made known to Lucius ere the stroke
Of this yet scarce-cold battle, at this instant
Is full accomplish'd; for the Roman eagle,
From south to west on wing soaring aloft,   472
Lessen'd herself, and in the beams o' the sun
So vanish'd: which foreshow'd our princely eagle,
The imperial Cæsar, should again unite
His favour with the radiant Cymbeline,   476
Which shines here in the west.
   Cym.   Laud we the gods;
And let our crooked smokes climb to their nostrils
From our bless'd altars. Publish we this peace
To all our subjects. Set we forward: let   480
A Roman and a British ensign wave
Friendly together; so through Lud's town march:
And in the temple of great Jupiter
Our peace we'll ratify; seal it with feasts.   484
Set on there. Never was a war did cease,
Ere bloody hands were wash'd, with such a peace.
                               Exeunt.

FINIS.

NOTES

I. i. 1-3. *our bloods No more obey the heavens than our courtiers Still seem as does the king.* Our dispositions are no more surely governed by the heavens, i.e. the stars, than are the looks of courtiers governed by the expression of the king.

I. i. 25. *extend him within himself.* 'My praise however extensive is within his merit.' (Johnson.)

I. i. 30, 31. According to Shakespeare, Cassibelan was Cymbeline's uncle, Tenantius Cymbeline's father. Holinshed gives a different genealogy.

I. i. 69. S. d. In the Folio this stage direction is the first in *Scena secunda*. Most modern editors make no change of scene, as there is no change of place or lapse of time.

I. i. 87. *Always reserv'd my holy duty.* Never forgetting my sacred filial duty of respect; the modern equivalent would be 'with all due respect to my dear father.'

I. i. 101. *Though ink be made of gall.* 'Though the accent falls metrically on *made* I prefer to place it on *be*.' (Furness.)

I. i. 104-106. *I never do him wrong But he does buy my injuries, to be friends Pays dear for my offences.* Whenever I do him wrong I make it appear that he has wronged me and force him to buy off my wrath; in order to be friends he is willing to assume the blame and pay dear for my offences.

I. i. 116, 117. *cere up my embracements from a next With bands of death.* Folio reads *sear up,* and many former editors have explained the phrase as meaning to dry up, cause to wither etc. Furness points out that the New English Dictionary gives *sear* as a sixteenth and seventeenth century form of *cere* (i.e. to wrap in a shroud of waxed cloth), and feels that the reference to the *bands of death* 'leaves no doubt that the word here alludes to the cerements of death.'

I. i. 146, 147. *overbuys me Almost the sum he pays.* 'That is, he gives himself, worth any woman, and gets in return only my almost worthless self.' (Rolfe.)

I. ii. 13, 14. 'In order to spare him, Posthumus's steel sneaked roundabout Cloten's body, like a debtor trying to avoid his creditors.' (Delius.) Possibly, however, the reference is to Cloten's sword and his awkwardness in fighting.

I. ii. 36, 37. The second lord plays on the word *sign*, interpreting it as constellation, and *reflection* as planetary influence.

I. iii. 4. *As offer'd mercy is.* The clause which ends with this phrase is a good example of Shakespeare's elliptical style in *Cymbeline.* Imogen's meaning is obvious, viz. the loss of a letter from Posthumus would be as hard to bear as the loss of a reprieve to a criminal (or possibly as the loss of God's mercy to a sinner).

I. iii. 17. *I would have broke mine eye-strings, crack'd them.* The eye-strings, or tendons of the eye, were supposed to crack at the loss of sight.

I. iii. 34-37. Utterly worthless are the guesses of editors as to what Imogen's two charming words would have been. As the north wind shakes the buds on the trees and so prevents their growing, so Cymbeline's anger prevents this bud of love from ripening further.

I. iv. 13, 14. Dowden quotes *3 Henry VI* II. i. 91, 92: 'Nay, if thou be that princely eagle's bird, Show thy descent by gazing 'gainst the sun.'

I. iv. 17, 18. *words him . . . a great deal from the matter.* 'Makes the description of him very distant from the truth.' (Johnson.)

I. iv. 20-22. *the approbation of those that weep this lamentable divorce under her colours are wonder-*

fully to extend him. The praise of Posthumus by those friends and followers of Imogen who bewail their separation (those that under her colors weep this lamentable divorce) tends greatly to increase his reputation. The obscurity of this sentence rises from the incorrect position of the phrase 'under her colours,' and from the plural verb 'are' where a singular is required.

I. iv. 50-52. *rather shunned to go even with what I heard than in my every action to be guided by others' experiences.* Posthumus means apparently that as a young man he preferred to avoid agreeing exactly with all that he heard to being guided in every action by the experience of others.

I. iv. 62, 63. *which may, without contradiction, suffer the report.* 'Which may, undoubtedly, be publicly told.' (Johnson.)

I. iv. 66, 67. *upon warrant of bloody affirmation.* 'Pledging himself to seal the truth of it with his blood.' (Rolfe.)

I. iv. 151. *a friend.* This is the First Folio reading and is intelligible: Iachimo says jocularly 'You are her friend and thus know her too well to risk much on her chastity.' Theobald altered *a friend* to *afraid* and in this reading has been followed by many editors.

I. iv. 171-173. *provided I have your commendation for my more free entertainment.* Provided that you will commend me to her generous hospitality.

I. v. 58. *To be depender on a thing that leans.* 'To be dependent on one who is himself dependent on others.' (Furness.) In the light of the two following lines Furness's interpretation seems less satisfactory than Johnson's, 'To be dependent on something that inclines towards its fall.'

I. vi. 6-9. *most miserable . . . comfort.* Those who have the most exalted desires are the most miserable of men (because their desires are likely to be unattainable) ; but happy are they, however humble, who

attain their simple desires, for the fact of attainment
gives a relish to (*seasons*) comfort.

I. vi. 20. *Parthian.* 'The ancient Parthian manner
of fighting was to shoot at an adversary while flying
or pretending to fly.' (Century Dictionary.)

I. vi. 34-38. *which can distinguish . . . foul.* Eyes
which can distinguish between one star and another
and between two stones of identical appearance as they
lie on the beach which is covered by numbers of them.
And with such precious spectacles (as our eyes) can we
not distinguish between fair and foul?

I. vi. 44-46. 'Desire when it approached sluttery,
and considered it in comparison with such neat excellence, would not only be not so allured to feed, but
seized with a fit of loathing would vomit emptiness,
would feel the convulsions of disgust, though, being
unfed, it had nothing to eject.' (Johnson.)

I. vi. 97, 98. *timely knowing, The remedy then
born.* 'Upon timely knowledge the remedy is
straightway born.' (Dowden.)

I. vi. 103, 104. *Takes prisoner . . . here.* 'From
her alone does the passion of my eye catch fire.'
(Dowden.) Many editors have followed the reading
of the later Folios which changed 'Fiering' of the First
Folio to 'Fixing.'

I. vi. 113-117. *Not I . . . out.* 'It is not I who
divulge the utter depths of his change, inclined though
I be to impart the news, but 'tis your loveliness that
has conjured up this report from the innermost silence
of my consciousness.' (Furness.) Probably 'inclined'
should rather be taken in the sense of 'because inclined.'

II. i. 2, 3. *when I kissed the jack, upon an up-cast to
be hit away.* The reference is to the game of bowls.
The jack is the small bowl at which the others are
aimed. The player 'kisses the jack' when his bowl

touches it without moving it. Cloten's bowl was knocked away from this advantageous position by another bowler who rolled straight up.

II. i. 12, 14. *curtail, crop.* The verb to curtail is from the obsolete word 'curtal,' meaning a horse with a docked tail; hence the second lord's feeble pun about cropping ears.

II. i. 26, 27. *capon . . . comb on.* Both these words refer probably to the fool's cap or coxcomb.

II. ii. 12. *Our Tarquin.* 'Our' because Iachimo is an Italian. The story of Tarquin is told by Shakespeare in *The Rape of Lucrece.*

II. ii. 13. *press the rushes.* Tread upon the rushes (which, in Shakespeare's own time, were strewn upon the floors).

II. ii. 17, 18. Iachimo longs to kiss Imogen's lips, 'rubies unparagon'd,' but obviously is not so foolhardy as to attempt it. The lips themselves do exquisitely, 'dearly,' what Iachimo longs to do.

II. ii. 22, 23. The white and azure refer to the white eyelids with their blue veins. Cf. Keats, *Eve of St. Agnes,* 'And still she slept an azure-lidded sleep.' In both cases 'the blue of heaven' in the eyelids of the sleeper is intended to denote her purity.

II. ii. 27. *contents o' the story.* Details of the story pictured on the arras.

II. ii. 34. *Gordian knot.* The knot tied by Gordius, king of Phrygia, which was so intricate that no one could untie it. An oracle declared that he who loosed it should be master of Asia. Alexander the Great cut it, and the oracle was fulfilled.

II. ii. 45. *The tale of Tereus.* Tereus married Procne. According to some versions of the myth, he tired of her, pretended she was dead, invited her sister Philomela to be his wife, ravished her, and tore out her tongue. Philomela contrived to communicate with Procne. Together they killed Itys, son of Tereus

and served him up in a dish for Tereus to eat. Tereus
was changed to a hawk, Procne to a swallow, Philomela
to a nightingale.

II. ii. 48, 49. *that dawning May bare the raven's
eye.* That dawn may open the eye of the raven, a bird
that wakes early.

II. ii. 51. *time.* Iachimo has heard Imogen ask to
be called at four. As the clock strikes he counts 'one,
two, three,' and on the fourth stroke shuts the lid of
the trunk saying, 'time, time.' (Ingleby.)

II. iii. 2, 3. *turned up ace.* The reference is to
cutting a pack of cards, upon which occasion only ace
is low. Ace and ass were pronounced alike: the first
lord is quibbling.

II. iii. 136. *south-fog.* 'Southerne winds vnbind
humours . . . & they cause heauinesse of wits of
feeling: they corrupt and destroye, they heat, and
maketh men fall into sicknesse. And they breed the
gout, the falling euill, itch, and the ague.' (*Batman
vppon Bartholme,* 1582, lib. xi, chap. 3, quoted by
Furness.) Compare *Coriolanus* I. iv. 30: 'All the con-
tagion of the south light on you!'

II. iv. 6-8. *in these fear'd hopes . . . debtor.* If
these hopes, which are mixed with fears, are realised,
I shall barely have enough to repay your affection; if
they are not realised, I shall die much in your debt.
Tyrwhitt's emendation, *seared* for *feared,* has been
followed by many editors.

II. iv. 24. *mingled with their courage.* The First
Folio reads 'wing-led with their courages.' Dowden
interprets this to mean that wings of their army are
led by courageous commanders. All the later Folios
correct *wing-led* to read *mingled,* but retain the plural
form of courage. The First Folio reading of this passage requires a rather ingenious but far-fetched interpretation.

II. iv. 73, 74. *strive In workmanship and value.*

In it the workmanship and the intrinsic value strive with each other for preëminence.

II. iv. 83. *likely to report themselves.* So lifelike that one might expect them to speak.

II. iv. 83-85. *the cutter . . . out.* 'The sculptor was as nature, but as nature dumb; he gave everything that nature gives but breath and motion.' (Johnson.)

III. i. 20. 'The sea is made by the figure of speech a park, and the rocks a fence of oaks that pale it in.' (Porter & Clark.)

III. ii. 34. *For it doth physic love.* 'Grief in absence keeps love in health and vigour.' (Johnson.)

III. ii. 36, 37. *Lovers And men in dangerous bonds pray not alike.* I.e. lovers bless the bees for the wax which seals their letters; prisoners curse the bees for the wax which seals their forfeited bonds.

III. ii. 42, 43. *as you . . . eyes.* A carelessly constructed sentence which a multitude of emendations and explanations makes no clearer. Posthumus seems to mean that a loving look from Imogen would renew and revive him, no matter how cruel the law and her father's wrath had been to him. Cf. Romeo: 'Look thou but sweet, And I am proof against their enmity.' (*Romeo and Juliet* II. ii. 72, 73.)

III. ii. 66. *Why should excuse be born or ere begot?* 'Why contrive an excuse before the act is done for which the excuse will be necessary?' (Malone.)

III. ii. 73, 74. *sands That run i' the clock's behalf.* 'Sands of the hour-glass that run instead of the clock.' (Collier.)

III. ii. 79-81. *I see . . . through.* I see only the course that lies directly before me. Everything else, here, and here, and beyond, is obscure.

III. iii. 16, 17. *This service . . . allow'd.* Belarius, in his involved style, is here, I think, expressing sentiments akin to those expressed more clearly in the *Collect for Peace* by the clause 'whose service is perfect freedom.' 'This servile labour of ours is not servile, being done as we do it, but being so done it is approved (*allowed*) or enjoyed by us.'

III. iii. 25, 26.   Such men receive deference from the tradesmen who made the finery, but their accounts are not cancelled (for all this deference). Theirs is no life compared with ours.

III. iii. 51.   *which dies i' the search.* Editors disagree about the antecedent of *which,* whether it is *pain,* or *name,* or *fame and honour.* The punctuation of the First Folio would indicate that *fame and honour* were not the antecedents, for there is a comma after *fame.* Whatever the antecedent, the general import of the sentence is clear.

III. iii. 96-98.   *in as like . . . conceiving.* 'That is, acting my words as graphically as his brother. While Guiderius's gestures reflect the immediate impression of Belarius's tale, Arviragus, a more imaginative hearer, heightens what he hears by his greater energy of conception.' (Herford.) *Figure* is used in the sense of an acted part, as in *Tempest* III. iii. 83.

III. iv. 52.   *Whose mother was her painting.* 'Who was born of her paint-box.' (Hudson.)

III. iv. 60, 61.   *Æneas, Sinon.* The reference is to Æneas's desertion of Dido, queen of Carthage; cf. Vergil's *Æneid,* Bk. IV. Sinon, a Greek, with tears and protests deceived the Trojans, and persuaded them to take the wooden horse, filled with Greek soldiers, into the city of Troy.

III. iv. 83.   *scriptures.* Imogen uses the word literally in reference to the letters of Posthumus, which she implies have been her 'sacred writings'; then she plays on the word, using Holy Scripture as a synonym of orthodoxy, as opposed to *heresy,* in the next line.

III. iv. 86.   *stomachers.* Again Imogen plays on

words. She removes Posthumus's letters from her bosom, saying that she will no more use them as *stomachers,* as ornamental breast-coverings, worn by women, were called; but she also has in mind the word *stomach* in its significance as *courage:* the letters of Posthumus will never again bring courage to her heart.

III. iv. 135. This line lacks one syllable in the Folios. Many editors, following Theobald, correct this defect in metre by adding the word *Cloten* to the end of the line. Porter and Clark, defending the Folio reading, suggest that the time of the missing word is filled up 'by Imogen's exasperated pause, when she can think of nothing bad enough further, except his name.'

III. iv. 140, 141. *I' the world's volume Our Britain seems as of it, but not in 't.* Britain seems like a page torn out of the volume; of it, but not in it.

III. iv. 177, 178. *which will make him know, If that his head have ear in music.* Pisanio is, I think, referring to the music of Imogen's voice. Your very telling of your accomplishments will, he says, make him realize one of them if he has a musical ear.

III. v. 9. *your Grace, and you.* Perhaps the *you* refers to Cloten, but I think not, for the farewell to Cloten seems to come in line 12; perhaps Lucius means to distinguish between the Queen and the woman, 'all joy to you as Queen and as woman'; or perhaps for *you* we should read *yours.*

III. vi. 7. *Foundations.* Used quibblingly for (1) things which are supposedly fixed and permanent, and (2) endowed institutions, such as hospitals. Compare the following clause, 'such, I mean, where they should be relieved.'

III. vi. 24. *Take or lend.* Take my life or give me food, *or* 'Take what I have before (*or* in the sense of *ere*) you give me food.' (Dowden.)

III. vi. 27. *Such a foe.* Heavens. grant me such a foe!

III. vi. 69, 70. *In honesty I bid for you, as I do buy.* Honorably I ask for your favor, as I would honorably pay for it.

III. vi. 84, 85. *laying by . . . multitudes.* Dispensing with the worthless tribute of fickle multitudes.

IV. ii. 29. *miracle.* The word seems to be used in the sense of *mystery,* and the sentence to mean: The identity of this youth who is loved before me is a mystery.

IV. ii. 59. *stinking-elder.* The elder was a tree of ill repute. Judas Iscariot was said to have hanged himself on an elder; black fungus droops from it; and both leaves and blossoms have an unpleasant odor.

IV. ii. 81. *my clothes.* Cloten is obviously referring to court apparel in general, not to the clothes of Posthumus which he is wearing.

IV. ii. 109-112. *Being scarce . . . fear.* Having scarcely the wits of a man, Cloten was not afraid even of 'roaring terrors' which would terrify an intelligent man, for defect of judgment is often the cause of (not *fear* as Shakespeare carelessly writes but) boldness. The Cambridge editors suggest that a line may have dropped out, and that the original sentence may have had the following purport: 'defect of judgment supplies the place of courage, while true judgment is oft the cause of fear.' Dowden's suggested emendation, *cease* for *cause,* though ingenious, is not convincing. *Cease* has not the true Shakespearean ring in this place.

IV. ii. 159-161. *I would . . . answer.* I wish that revenges would seek us out and call us to account, that we might meet them with all possible strength.

IV. ii. 252. *Thersites' body is as good as Ajax'.* Thersites, the most deformed in body and mind of all the Greeks at the siege of Troy. Ajax, a Greek warrior, gigantic in body and of great courage. Cf. *Troilus and Cressida.*

IV. ii. 285. *Upon . . . faces.* This is apparently a direction from Belarius to scatter the flowers upon the faces of Imogen and Cloten; but Cloten's body is headless. Did Shakespeare forget?

IV. ii. 310, 311. His foot as nimble and graceful as that of Mercury, his thigh as mighty as that of Mars, his arms as strong as those of Hercules, his face as majestic as that of Jove. These references to the gods explain the first phrase in the next line, 'Murder in heaven!'

IV. ii. 313. *Hecuba.* Wife of Priam, king of Troy. In the player's recitation in *Hamlet* (II. ii. 544 ff.), Shakespeare refers to 'the instant burst of clamor that she made' 'when she saw Pyrrhus . . . mincing . . . her husband's limbs.'

IV. ii. 364, 365. *otherwise . . . picture.* 'Nature took away the life—who mutilated the body?' (Dowden.)

IV. iii. 29. *Your preparation can affront no less.* Your army is prepared to face as many.

V. i. 15. *And make them dread it, to the doers' thrift.* None of the many proposed emendations of this line seems necessary. Posthumus means that the sinner who is allowed to 'second ills with ills' begins to dread a future of continuous degeneration, and this fear is 'thrift' or profitable to the 'doer' or sinner.

V. iii. 25-28. *Stand . . . frown.* Stand, or we will play the part of the Romans and will give you that beastly death which, like beasts, you are shunning and from which you may save yourselves by looking back defiantly upon the enemy.

V. iii. 42, 43. *slaves, The strides they victors made.* This clause is parallel in construction to the preceding one. Those who came as eagles fled as chickens; those who came as victors fled as slaves.

V. iv. 1. *You shall not now be stol'n, you have locks upon you.* 'The wit of the Gaoler alludes to the custom of putting a lock on a horse's leg when he is turned out to pasture.' (Johnson.)

V. iv. 11-17. Posthumus here soliloquizes on the three steps which man must take to receive pardon and absolution, viz. contrition (l. 11), penance (ll. 13-15), and satisfaction (ll. 16, 17). The meaning of the first four lines is clear. Line 15, *Desir'd more than constrain'd,* refers to the gyves, symbols of his voluntary penance; ll. 15, 16 signify that if satisfaction, *to satisfy,* be the main part of salvation, *freedom,* from sin, then the gods may take no less than all which he has and is, if thereby he may be freed.

V. iv. 26. *You rather . . . yours.* Men do not weigh every coin they receive, but accept them because of their 'image and superscription'; so, although my life is not so valuable as Imogen's, yet the gods made it in their image and should the more readily, i.e. *rather,* take it in compensation.

V. iv. 156. *well cooked.* The reference is to meat which is hung up, either preparatory to cooking or instead of being cooked.

V. iv. 158. *the dish . . . shot.* 'The viands (namely, himself) pay the reckoning.' (Furness.)

V. iv. 214. *hath a preferment.* Includes a hope for my own advancement.

V. v. 166. *Postures beyond brief nature.* Beauties of form that surpass those created by hasty Nature.

V. v. 168. *hook of wiving.* Physical beauty, the hook wherewith wives catch husbands.

V. v. 304-306. *hath More of thee merited than a band of Clotens Had ever scar for.* Guiderius deserves more from the king than a whole band of men like Cloten for actions for which they have been scarred in battle.

V. v. 354, 355. *The service that you three have done is more Unlike than this thou tell'st.* 'I have the less reason to be incredulous because the actions you have done within my knowledge are more incredible than the story you relate.' (Johnson.)

V. v. 385. *Distinction should be rich in.* A clearer statement should bring out fully.

V. v. 397, 398. *the counterchange Is severally in all.* 'This is reciprocated by all.' (Rolfe.)

APPENDIX A

SOURCES OF THE PLAY

The name Cymbeline, and the political setting of the play, Shakespeare took from Holinshed's *Chronicles of England*. The wager-story, which forms the basis of the Imogen plot, is a familiar one in mediæval literature; Shakespeare seems to have been chiefly indebted for this story to the ninth novel of the second day in Boccaccio's *Decameron*. It is hardly likely that he was familiar with an English version of this story, published possibly in 1603 but probably not before 1620, called *Westward for Smelts*. Other versions of the story which Shakespeare may, or may not, have known in some sixteenth century English form, are the thirteenth century French romances, *King Florus and Fair Jehane*,[1] *Roman de la Violette*, and *Roman del conte de Poitiers;* a fourteenth century French mystery play; as well as scattered German, Scandinavian, and Gaelic versions. An English play printed in 1589, called *The Rare Triumphs of Love and Fortune*, may have suggested some names, characters, and incidents for *Cymbeline, The Winter's Tale,* and *The Tempest*. Beaumont and Fletcher's *Philaster* resembles *Cymbeline* in many details; the two plays were written at about the same time, and it is impossible to state definitely which influenced the other. Both plays indicate that a new type of drama was becoming fashionable toward the end of the first decade of the seventeenth century; it is quite conceivable that they were written contemporaneously and in friendly

[1] English translation in *Aucassin and Nicolette and Other Mediæval Romances*, Everyman's Library Edition, E. F Dutton.

rivalry. The story of Belarius and the kidnapped princes, as well as the final solution of the complicated plot, seems to have been Shakespeare's own invention.[1]

Cimbeline, or Kymbeline, was, according to Holinshed, a descendant of King Lear, and reigned in Britain from 33 B. C. to 2 A. D. He had been educated in Rome and 'knighted' by Cæsar Augustus. His sons were Guiderius and Arviragus. 'Our histories do affirme' that Cymbeline, and his father Tenantius (cf. *Cymbeline* I. i. 31) before him, lived at peace with the Romans, 'and continuallie to them paied the tributes which the Britaines had couenanted with Julius Cæsar to paie, yet we find in the Romane writers that after Julius Cæsar's death . . . the Britaines refused to paie that tribute: whereat Augustus, being otherwise occupied, was content to winke; howbeit . . . at length . . . Augustus made prouision to passe with an armie ouer into Britaine, & was come forward vpon his iournie into Gallia Celtica. . . . But here receiuing aduertisements that the Pannonians . . . and the Dalmatians . . . had rebelled (cf. *Cymbeline* III. i. 73-75), he thought it best first to subdue those rebells neere home.' Holinshed is at a loss to know whether to believe 'our histories' or 'the Romane writers,' but he records presently the arrival of an ambassador from Augustus at the court of Cymbeline, who came to bring to the British king the thanks of the emperor 'for that he had kept his allegiance toward the Romane empire.' Later, Guiderius, after his accession, refused to pay a yearly tribute of three thousand crowns. Shakespeare, by attributing this refusal to Cymbeline, hoped to heighten the dramatic and emotional appeal of this singularly mild and uneventful portion of Holinshed's *Chronicle*.

[1] For more detailed discussion of these points see Thorndike: *Influence of Beaumont and Fletcher on Shakespeare*, Worcester, Massachusetts, 1901, and Dowden: *Cymbeline*, in *The Arden Shakespeare*, third edition, London, 1918.

Posthumus's account of the means whereby the British gained the victory (V. iii. 3-58) is taken from Holinshed's *Chronicles of Scotland,* which describe the sudden defeat of the Danes by the Scots, in the year 976, through the intervention of a husbandman named Hay, and his two sons.

The plot of Boccaccio's novel may be summarized as follows: Bernabo Lomellino of Genoa, stopping at an inn in Paris, boasts of his wife's virtue and devotion. Ambrogiuolo of Piacenza sneers at woman's virtue, and proves by philosophical argument that all women must be unchaste. Man is not chaste; woman is more frail than man; ergo! Entreaty, flattery, and gifts will win any woman. Bernabo repudiates philosophical argument and reaffirms his faith in his wife, Ginevra. The discussion waxes hot. Bernabo, in his anger, wagers his head against a thousand florins that Ambrogiuolo could not tempt Ginevra to sin. Ambrogiuolo accepts the wager, substituting a sum of money for Bernabo's head, and starts for Genoa. Within three months he must return with indisputable proofs of his triumph over Ginevra's virtue. Just as he is despairing of success he meets a poor woman, to whom Ginevra has been kind, and bribes her to send him into Ginevra's chamber, in her chest, on the pretence that she is about to take a journey and wishes to leave her belongings in Ginevra's care. Night comes; he emerges from the chest, notes the situation of the room, its ornaments and pictures, and approaching the bed he admires the lady's beauty and perceives the mole on her left breast. For further evidence he removes a gown, a ring, and a girdle. Bernabo is not moved by the description of the room, nor by the articles of apparel, but is 'struck to the very heart' when Ambrogiuolo reveals his knowledge of the mole. He sets out for home 'most cruelly incensed against his wife,' and sends ahead a servant with a letter asking Ginevra to meet him on the way. The servant is instructed to murder her when he reaches 'a fit place.' Ginevra persuades the servant to let her escape, disguised as a page, and to carry word to his lord that she is dead. As page to a Catalonian lord she sails for foreign lands, and on her journeys encounters Ambrogiuolo and hears him tell, as a jest, the story of his wager. She arranges to have her husband brought over seas to listen as Ambrogiuolo tells this tale to the Sultan. The truth is then revealed, and after the Sultan has condemned Ambrogiuolo to be smeared with honey and eaten by wasps,[1] they all sit down to a sumptuous banquet. It is only in the early part of the tale, the long-drawn-out angry debate which provides some possible motivation for the story, that Boccaccio's plot surpasses Shakespeare's.

APPENDIX B

HISTORY OF THE PLAY

Cymbeline was first printed in 1623, at the end of the First Folio, among the tragedies, and under the title, *The Tragedie of Cymbeline*. The text was taken from a prompt-book copy, and was divided into acts and scenes; but it was so carelessly printed that it is full of obscure and perplexing readings. In this play Shakespeare seems to have had the assistance of a coadjutor, who was responsible for the Vision of Posthumus in Act V, which is not an integral part of the action, and perhaps for portions of the Belarius plot.

[1] This episode of the honey and the wasps, not used by Shakespeare in *Cymbeline*, is probably the source of the passage in *The Winter's Tale* (IV. iv. 816 ff.) in which Autolycus threatens the Clown with a similar fate.

The play was probably first produced in 1610; in style, diction, and versification it resembles the two romantic comedies, *The Winter's Tale* and *The Tempest,* which appeared in 1610 and 1611, respectively. Dr. Simon Forman, astrologer, quack, and theatre-goer, who in his *Book of Plays* kept a record of the plays he attended, gives a synopsis of the plot of '*Cimbalin*' in an undated entry which follows an entry dated May 15, 1611, recording a performance of '*The Winters Talle*' at the glob.' On January 1, 1633/4, '*Cymbeline* was acted at court by the King's players. Well likte by the Kinge.'[1]

Irreverent hands were laid upon *Cymbeline* in 1682 by Tom Durfey, who attempted to fashion it to the taste of his generation under the title, *The Injured Princess or The Fatal Wager*. The names of the characters are changed—Imogen becomes Eugenia, Posthumus is Ursaces, and Iachimo is Shatillion; new characters are introduced, among them Clarina, who is Eugenia's confidante and daughter of Pisanio, and a drunken friend of Cloten's named Iachimo. Pisanio believes in Imogen's guilt; the lascivious Cloten and his ribald friend kidnap Clarina with evil intent; there is little left of Shakespeare's play but the outline of the plot. This perversion of *Cymbeline* held the stage until 1720, when Shakespeare's play was produced at the new Lincoln's Inn Fields Theatre.

But in 1755 another attempt was made, by Charles Marsh, to refashion the 'old and crude' play; and in 1759 still another. This time the culprit was the Professor of Poetry at Oxford, William Hawkins, M.A., who possessed 'so thorough a veneration for the great Father of the English stage' that he 'retained, in many places, the very language of the original

[1] *Dramatic Records of Sir Henry Herbert, Master of the Revels 1623-1673,* edited by J. Q. Adams, Yale University Press, 1917.

author.' Fortunately 'unprecedented difficulties and discouragements in the theatre' prevented a long run at Covent Garden Theatre. Two years later, in 1761, Garrick made the first of his many appearances as Posthumus in Shakespeare's play. The play ran for sixteen nights, and the *Dramatic Censor* stated that Garrick's astonishing talents were never more happily exerted. In 1767 and 1770 Mrs. Barry played Imogen to Garrick's Posthumus. John Philip Kemble first played Posthumus in 1785; Mrs. Siddons first appeared as Imogen in 1787; and Charles Kemble, who had appeared as Polydore in 1812 played Posthumus in 1825. Macready played Posthumus in 1818. From the time of Garrick on, *Cymbeline* seems to have been a favorite play for one-night, benefit performances. Helen Faucit was one of the great Imogens of the middle of the nineteenth century, and Ellen Terry's 'last great part on the Lyceum stage' was the rôle of Imogen in Henry Irving's gorgeous production in 1896. Irving chose to play the part of Iachimo, and seems to have made an indifferent success in the rôle. Popular enthusiasm was devoted to Miss Terry's Imogen and to the setting by Alma Tadema.

While Garrick and the Kembles were using *Cymbeline* almost yearly in England, the new and struggling theatres in the American colonies and states followed their illustrious example. From 1767 to 1793 eight revivals of *Cymbeline* occurred along our Atlantic seaboard, three in New York, two in Philadelphia, one in Boston, one in Annapolis, and one in Charleston, South Carolina. One hundred years later *Cymbeline* again became popular on the American stage. Mary Shaw Hamblin, who died in 1873, was a famous Imogen in the sixties. Adelaide Neilson in the seventies, Modjeska in the eighties, and Margaret Mather in the nineties kept the play familiar to American audiences. In 1906 Viola Allen again revived it, and in 1923 Edward H. Sothern and Julia Marlowe added it to their repertoire.[1]

APPENDIX C

THE TEXT OF THE PRESENT EDITION

The text of the present edition is, by permission of the Oxford University Press, based on that of the Oxford Shakespeare, edited by the late W. J. Craig. Stage directions, when not bracketed, are from the First Folio; bracketed stage directions are modern.

In the following list of variants from the Oxford text, the readings of this edition precede, and Craig's readings follow, the colon. The Folio authority is given wherever involved.

I. i. 116	cere: sear Ff
I. i. 117	bands: bonds Ff
I. i. 132	heap'st Ff: heap'st instead
I. iv. 68	constant-qualified: constant, qualified **Ff**
I. iv. 151	a friend Ff: afraid
I. iv. 177	understand Ff: understand that
I. v. 68	change thou chancest: chance thou changest **Ff**
I. v. 83	primroses: prime-roses Ff
I. vi. 22	*Imo. reads* Ff: *Imo.*
I. vi. 24	trust Ff: truest
I. vi. 122	self exhibition Ff1, 4: self-exhibition Ff2, 3
II. ii. 32	sense Ff: senses
II. iii. 126	foil Ff: soil
II. iv. 6	fear'd Ff: sear'd
II. iv. 21	order'd Ff: ordered
II. iv. 24	mingled Ff2, 3, 4 (F1 wing-led): winged
II. iv. 75	So rarely Ff: rarely
II. v. 2	bastards Ff: bastards all
II. v. 27	may be named Ff2, 3, 4 (F1 name): man may name

[1] For details concerning the various stage adaptations of the play see Fr. Lücke, *Über Bearbeitungen von Shakespeares 'Cymbeline'* (Rostock diss., 1909).

III. i. 20   oaks Ff: rocks
III.ii.42,43 would even Ff: would not even
III. iv. 104 mine eyeballs Ff: mine eyeballs blind
III. iv. 135 nothing: F1 nothing; F2 nothing? Ff3, 4
              nothing Cloten
III. iv. 177 will Ff: you'll
III. v. 9   your Grace, and you Ff: your Grace. *Qu.* And
              you!
III. v. 44   the loudest of (th' lowd of Ff): the loudest
III. v. 95   once, Ff: once
III. vi. 73   After long absence Ff: After a long absence
IV. i. 21   happily Ff: haply
IV. ii. 112   cause of fear Ff: cease of fear
IV. ii. 170   thou thyself F1 (thyself Ff2, 3, 4): how thyself
IV. ii. 207   but ay: but I Ff
IV. ii. 237   to our mother Ff: our mother
V. i. 20   mistress; peace Ff: mistress-piece
V. iii. 92   leg Ff: lag
V. iv. 60   Leonati Ff: Leonati's
V. v. 393   interrogatories Ff: inter-gatories

APPENDIX D

Suggestions for Collateral Reading

I. Editions.

E. Dowden: *The Arden Shakespeare,* 1903 (3d ed., 1918).

H. H. Furness: *The Variorum Shakespeare,* 1913.

II. General Criticism.

W. Hazlitt: *Characters of Shakespeare's Plays,* 1817. Everyman's Library edition, pp. 1-11.

Lady Martin: *On Some of Shakespeare's Female Characters,* 1885.

Barrett Wendell: *William Shakespeare, a Study in Elizabethan Literature,* 1894, pp. 355-364.

F. S. Boas: *Shakespeare and His Predecessors,* 1895, pp. 504-517.

G. Brandes: *William Shakespeare, a Critical Study,* 1898, pp. 615-634.

L. A. Sherman: *What Is Shakespeare?* 1902, pp. 9-110.

G. F. Baker: *The Development of Shakespeare as a Dramatist,* 1907, pp. 293-295.

J. Masefield: *Shakespeare,* 1911, pp. 223-226.

A. Symons: *Studies in the Elizabethan Drama,* 1919, pp. 132-146.

W. W. Lawrence: *The Wager in Cymbeline.* Publications of the Modern Language Association, December, 1920.

R. M. Alden: *Shakespeare,* 1922. Chapter vii.

INDEX OF WORDS GLOSSED

(Figures in full-faced type refer to page-numbers)

heaviness: **103** (V. ii. 1)
Hecuba: **94** (IV. ii. 313)
Hercules: **93** (IV. ii. 311)
hilding: **40** (II. iii. 128)
hind: **107** (V. iii. 77)
hold: **57** (III. iii. 20); **98** (IV. iii. 16)
holy: **4** (I. i. 87)
home: **72** (III. v. 92)
honest: **22** (I. vi. 8)
honour: **2** (I. i. 29)
hoodwink'd: **104** (V. ii. 16)
hook: **122** (V. v. 168)
horse-hairs: **37** (II. iii. 33)
humour: **22** (I. v. 81)
hunt: **78** (III. vi. 89)

illustrous: **27** (I. vi. 109)
imperceiverant: **80** (IV. i. 15)
importance: **14** (I. iv. 47)
importantly: **100** (IV. iv. 19)
inclin'd: **27** (I. vi. 114)
inform: **4** (I. i. 79)
inherit: **55** (III. ii. 62)
injurious: **52** (III. i. 48)
intelligence: **27** (I. vi. 114)
into: **29** (I. vi. 167)
irregulous: **94** (IV. ii. 315)
issues: **32** (II. i. 53)
it: **66** (III. iv. 160)

jack: **31** (II. i. 2)
jackanapes: **31** (II. i. 4)
Jack-slave: **31** (II. i. 23)
jay: **62** (III. iv. 51)
jealousy: **98** (IV. iii. 22)
jet: **57** (III. iii. 5)
join: **2** (I. i. 29)
journal: **81** (IV. ii. 10)
Jovial: **93** (IV. ii. 311)
jump: **115** (V. iv. 187)

keep: **53** (III. i. 73)
keep house: **56** (III. iii. 1)

ken: **75** (III. vi. 6)
kissed: **31** (II. i. 2)
knowing: **13** (I. iv. 31)
knowledge: **3** (I. i. 60)
known together: **13** (I. iv. 38)

labour: **74** (III. v. 168)
laboursome: **67** (III. iv. 167)
lamenting: **89** (IV. ii. 193)
laming: **122** (V. v. 164)
lapp'd: **130** (V. v. 361)
lapse: **75** (III. vi. 12)
lay: **17** (I. iv. 164)
lay out: **39** (II. iii. 92)
laying by: **78** (III. vi. 84)
lean'd: **4** (I. i. 78)
leaping-time: **89** (IV. ii. 200)
learn'd: **19** (I. v. 12)
leave: **16** (I. iv. 114)
left: **11** (I. iii. 14); **33** (II. ii. 4)
lend: **75** (III. vi. 24)
liegers: **22** (I. v. 80)
life: **106** (V. iii. 45)
like: **38** (II. iii. 59); **44** (II. iv. 36); **58** (III. iii. 41); **91** (IV. ii. 237)
likely: **45** (II. iv. 83)
limb-meal: **48** (II. iv. 147)
limit: **58** (III. iii. 35)
line: **38** (II. iii. 72)
livers: **66** (III. iv. 143)
loathness: **5** (I. i. 108)
locks: **108** (V. iv. 1)
long of: **126** (V. v. 272)
Lucina: **110** (V. iv. 43)
Lud's town: **51** (III. i. 32)

made: **43** (II. iv. 30); **123** (V. v. 183)
makes: **12** (I. iv. 10); **24** (I. vi. 38)
manner'd: **29** (I. vi. 166)